TALK WITH POWER TO ANYONE

UNLOCK THE SECRETS OF CONFIDENT COMMUNICATION, CRUSH INSECURITIES, BUILD GENUINE CONNECTIONS AND TRANSFORM YOUR SOCIAL LIFE FOREVER!

ISABEL PIERCE

ABOUT THE AUTHOR

Isabel Pierce is an author, speaker, and coach dedicated to helping people overcome their insecurities. As a naturally shy and introverted person herself, Isabel struggled for years to feel confident and comfortable in social situations, instead of giving up, she decided to turn her "weaknesses" into strengths.

Isabel spent countless hours studying psychology, communication, and personal development to better understand the nature of shyness and introversion. She also pushed herself out of her comfort zone and challenged herself to practice socializing and networking.

With years of experience and research under her belt, Isabel now shares her knowledge and expertise with others. Through her coaching and workshops, she helps people develop the skills and confidence they need to thrive in social situations.

Isabel's mission is to empower anyone to realize their full potential and live the life they desire. She believes that everyone deserves to feel confident and comfortable in their own skin, and that with the right tools and mindset, everyone can push their limits.

TABLE OF CONTENTS

INTRODUCTION

"Our biggest communication problem is that we don't listen to understand. We listen to respond."

Stephen R. Covey

This quote by Stephen R. Covey resonates with us all. We've all experienced those moments when we feel like we're talking to a brick wall or not connecting with someone the way we hoped. Communication is a complex and ever-evolving skill critical to our personal and professional lives, yet many of us don't give it the attention it deserves. It's time to change that.

In today's fast-paced world, effective communication has become more critical. With the advent of technology, we're now communicating with people worldwide at the click of a button. We're interacting with people from different cultures and backgrounds, and we must understand how to communicate with them effectively.

Connecting with others is not just a valuable skill; it's a necessity. Whether in business or navigating your relationships, being a good communicator is vital to success. It can mean the difference between getting that job you want, closing that important deal, or building meaningful relationships with the people in your life.

That's where "HOW TO TALK TO ANYONE AND INCREASE YOUR LEVEL OF EMPATHY" comes in. This practical guide is designed to help you become a better communicator, capable of connecting with any person and succeeding in any conversation. Whether you're looking to ace that job interview, make a new friend, or want to be more confident in social situations, this book has got you covered.

In the following chapters, we'll explore the art of communication and explore the techniques and strategies to help you become a better communicator. We'll cover various topics, from building a solid foundation for confident communication to understanding the power of empathy and the nuances of nonverbal communication. We'll also explore the intricacies of small talk and delve into digital communication.

But this isn't just any ordinary self-help book. This is a guide that will help you transform the way you communicate and connect with people. It's about understanding that communication is more than just words – it's about listening actively, reading body language, and understanding the emotions and needs of the person you're speaking with.

Throughout the pages of this book, you'll find practical exercises, real-life examples, and expert insights that will help you build your communication skills and achieve your goals. We'll share stories of people who have transformed their lives by learning to communicate effectively and show you how you can do the same.

But this book is not just about building connections with others. It's also about making a stronger connection with yourself. We'll help you develop the confidence and self-awareness you need to communicate quickly and authentically and show you how to tap into your inner strengths to become a better communicator.

In conclusion, effective communication is an essential skill that can help you succeed in all aspects of your life. By learning to connect with others, you can achieve your goals, build meaningful relationships, and create a more fulfilling life. This book will help you become a better communicator and tap into your full potential. So, take a deep breath, open your mind, and get ready to embark on a journey of self-discovery and transformation. Together, we can unlock the power of communication and learn how to talk to anyone with confidence and empathy.

So, this book is for you whether you're a shy introvert or a confident extrovert, whether you're in sales or marketing, or whether you want to improve your relationships. We invite you to join us on this journey of discovery and transformation, to learn the art of communication and become the best communicator. Are you ready to take the first step? Let's begin.

LAYING THE FOUNDATION FOR A CONFIDENT YOU

Have you ever experienced the frustration of stumbling over your words during a crucial conversation? Perhaps you found yourself struggling to articulate your thoughts clearly or unable to express yourself as you intended. These moments can be incredibly frustrating and can leave you feeling powerless and disconnected from others.

Effective communication is about more than just finding the right words to say. It's about building a solid foundation for confident communication, encompassing your words and thoughts, beliefs, and emotions underpinning them. This chapter will dive into the critical elements of building self-assurance and overcoming limiting beliefs that might hinder your communication skills.

You'll learn how to cultivate a growth mindset, manage anxiety, and improve your body language - all essential to becoming a confident communicator. With practical tips and techniques, we'll guide you through developing the skills you need to feel confident and self-assured in any conversation. So, if you're ready to take your communication skills to the next level, let's get started.

RECOGNIZING AND OVERCOMING LIMITING BELIEFS

Building a solid foundation for confident communication begins with recognizing and overcoming limiting beliefs. Limiting beliefs are those negative thoughts and ideas about ourselves and our abilities, which can hinder our potential and undermine our confidence. To overcome limiting beliefs, we must identify and challenge them.

Here are the steps to recognizing and overcoming limiting beliefs:

1. Identify your limiting beliefs: Reflect on your thoughts and ideas about yourself and your abilities. Write down any negative reviews that come to mind. Be honest with yourself, and don't hold back.

2. Challenge your limiting beliefs: Once you have identified them, it's time to challenge them. Ask yourself if these beliefs are based on facts or just assumptions. Are they helping you or holding you back? Be objective and try to view the situation from a different perspective.

3. Replace negative thoughts with positive affirmations: Replace your negative thoughts with positive affirmations. Focus on your strengths and accomplishments. Remind yourself of your successes and how capable you are.

4. Practice self-compassion: Be kind to yourself and practice self-compassion. Recognize that everyone has flaws and makes

mistakes and that it's okay not to be perfect. Treat yourself with the kindness and understanding you would offer a friend.

These steps can overcome limiting beliefs and build a strong foundation for confident communication. Remember, communication is not just about the words you speak; it's also about the confidence you exude.

DEVELOPING A GROWTH MINDSET

Developing a growth mindset is not an overnight process but worth the effort. Here are some steps to help you cultivate a growth mindset:

1.   Embrace challenges: Feeling overwhelmed and defeated is easy when you encounter challenges. However, challenges present an opportunity for growth and learning. Instead of shying away from challenges, embrace them as opportunities to improve your skills.

2.   View failures as learning opportunities: Failure is a natural learning process. Instead of viewing failure as a sign of weakness or incompetence, use it as a chance to learn and improve. Ask yourself, "What can I learn from this experience?" and "How can I do better next time?"

3.   Surround yourself with positive influences: The people you surround yourself with significantly impact your mindset. Seek out individuals who inspire and motivate you, and avoid those who bring you down or discourage you.

4.   Practice self-compassion: Developing a growth mindset requires patience and self-compassion. Be kind to yourself, acknowledge your progress, and celebrate your successes, no matter how small they may seem.

By implementing these steps, you can cultivate a growth mindset and develop the belief that your abilities and intelligence are not fixed but can be improved over time with hard work and dedication.

TECHNIQUES FOR MANAGING ANXIETY

Anxiety is a common experience that can interfere with confident communication. It is characterized by unease, worry, or apprehension that can manifest physically or emotionally. Anxiety can arise in various situations, such as public speaking, job interviews, or difficult conversations. To manage anxiety and communicate confidently, it's essential to have a plan in place. Here are four techniques for managing anxiety that can help you feel more at ease:

1.   Recognize the Physical Symptoms of Anxiety: One of the first steps in managing anxiety is to become aware of the physical sensations that accompany it. These can include a rapid heartbeat, sweating, shaking, and shortness of breath. By recognizing these symptoms, you can take action to calm your body and mind.

2.   Practice Deep Breathing Exercises: Deep breathing is a simple yet effective way to reduce anxiety. It involves inhaling

deeply through your nose and exhaling slowly through your mouth. This helps to slow your heart rate and calm your mind. Try taking a few deep breaths before a stressful situation, or practice breathing exercises regularly to help reduce overall anxiety.

3.   Use Visualization Techniques: A visualization is a powerful tool for managing anxiety. It involves creating a mental image of yourself succeeding in a particular situation, such as delivering a successful presentation or acing a job interview. You can boost your confidence and reduce anxiety by imagining a positive outcome.

4.   Seek Professional Help: If your anxiety is severe or interfering with your daily life, it may be beneficial to seek professional help. A therapist or counselor can work with you to develop coping strategies and provide support as you navigate difficult situations.

By using these techniques for managing anxiety, you can feel more in control of your emotions and better equipped to communicate confidently. Remember, anxiety is a normal part of the human experience, and with practice, you can learn to manage it effectively.

BUILDING SELF-ESTEEM

Building self-esteem is an ongoing process that requires dedication and effort. Here are some practical steps you can take to boost your self-esteem and build a strong foundation for confident communication:

1.   Focus on your strengths and accomplishments: It's easy to get caught up in negative self-talk and focus on your weaknesses, but this can harm your self-esteem. Instead, list your strengths and accomplishments, no matter how small they may seem. Celebrate your successes and remind yourself of what you're capable of.

2.   Practice self-care: Taking care of yourself physically and emotionally is crucial for building self-esteem. Make sure you're getting enough rest, exercise, and proper nutrition. Take time to do the things that bring you joy and make you feel good.

3.   Surround yourself with positive and supportive people: The people you surround yourself with can significantly impact your self-esteem. Seek out friends and colleagues who are positive and supportive and who believe in you and your abilities. Avoid people who are negative, critical, or bring you down.

4.   Challenge negative self-talk: Negative self-talk can significantly hinder building self-esteem. When you catch yourself thinking negative thoughts about yourself, challenge them. Ask yourself if they're true, and try reframing them more positively.

By taking these steps, you can build self-esteem and develop a stronger foundation for confident communication. Building self-esteem is an ongoing process, so be patient and kind to yourself as you work towards your goals.

IMPROVING BODY LANGUAGE

Improving your body language is a vital part of becoming a confident communicator. Body language can convey much about your emotions, intentions, and confidence level. Here are some steps you can take to improve your body language:

1.   Stand up straight: Good posture is essential for conveying confidence. When you stand up straight, you appear taller and more assertive. Keep your shoulders back and your head up.

2.   Maintain eye contact: Eye contact is a powerful tool for building trust and conveying confidence. When you make eye contact with someone, you show that you are present and engaged in the conversation.

3.   Use open gestures: Open gestures, such as keeping your arms at your sides or gesturing with your palms up, convey confidence and openness. Avoid crossing your arms or legs, as this can make you appear defensive or closed off.

4.   Mirror the other person's body language: Mirroring the body language of the person you speak with can help build rapport and create a sense of connection. Pay attention to their posture, gestures, and facial expressions, and try to mirror them subtly.

5.   Avoid fidgeting: Fidgeting, such as playing with your hair or tapping your foot, can convey nervousness or discomfort. Try to keep your movements calm and deliberate.

Following these steps can improve your body language and convey confidence and openness in your communication. Remember, effective communication is more than words - it's about presenting yourself and connecting with others.

In a world where communication is vital to success, it's essential to have a strong foundation for confident communication. The techniques discussed in this chapter may seem small, but they lay the groundwork for becoming a powerful communicator. You can unlock your full potential and become your best communicator by recognizing and overcoming limiting beliefs, developing a growth mindset, managing anxiety, building self-esteem, and improving body language. So, take these tools and run with them - the journey to becoming a confident communicator starts here.

FIRST IMPRESSIONS ARE EVERYTHING

Have you ever walked into a room full of strangers and felt like all eyes were on you? The truth is, we all have. The first few seconds of meeting someone can set the tone for the interaction. That's why knowing how to make a positive first impression is crucial. In this chapter, we'll dive deep into the importance of first impressions, body language dos and don'ts, the strategies for making a lasting impression, how to dress for success, and the power of a confident handshake. You'll learn how to create a solid first impression that leaves a lasting impact and opens doors to endless opportunities. Get ready to transform how you present yourself, and watch as the world opens up.

THE IMPORTANCE OF FIRST IMPRESSIONS

First impressions are everything. Within seconds of meeting someone new, people start to form opinions about who you are, what you stand for, and whether they want to continue engaging with you. Research suggests that people form first impressions in as little as seven seconds, and it's hard to change those initial perceptions once they're established.

The importance of making a positive first impression cannot be overstated. A positive first impression can help you build connections, make new friends, secure job interviews, and advance your career. On the other hand, a negative first impression can hinder your progress and damage your reputation.

To make a positive first impression, being mindful of your appearance, behavior, and body language is essential. You want to present yourself in a way that conveys confidence, competence, and professionalism. Here are some tips to help you make a positive first impression:

1.   Be on time: Punctuality is a sign of respect and professionalism. Arrive early to meetings, interviews, and social events to give yourself enough time to settle in and prepare.

2.   Dress appropriately: Dress according to the occasion, whether a job interview, a networking event, or a casual meet-up. Make sure your clothes fit well, are clean and pressed, and match the level of formality of the event.

3.   Practice good body language: Your body language can speak volumes about your confidence and level of comfort. Stand tall, make eye contact, and smile warmly to show you're engaged and approachable.

4.   Be aware of your tone: Your voice can influence how others perceive you. Speak confidently and positively to show that you're confident and in control.

5.   Show genuine interest: Engage in active listening, ask thoughtful questions, and show interest in what others say. This will make them feel valued and appreciated, creating a positive impression.

By mastering these techniques, you'll be well on your way to making a positive first impression and creating meaningful connections with others. Remember, your first impression can open doors and create opportunities, so make it count.

BODY LANGUAGE DO'S AND DON'TS

Body language is a crucial aspect of communication that often goes unnoticed, yet it plays a significant role in making a positive first impression. Your body language communicates confidence, openness, and interest in the conversation. To ensure you're presenting your best self, here are some body language do's and don'ts you should consider:

1.	Posture: The way you hold yourself says a lot about you. A slouched posture communicates low confidence, while standing up straight and tall indicates you're confident and assertive. Ensure you're sitting or standing up straight and your shoulders are relaxed.

2.	Eye Contact: Making eye contact is a sign of respect and interest in the conversation. However, too much eye contact can be intimidating and uncomfortable for the other person. Aim for natural eye contact, which means looking at the other person about 60-70% of the time during the conversation.

3.	Gestures are essential to body language but can also be distracting if they're excessive or inappropriate. Use hand gestures to emphasize your points, but ensure they're natural and not forced.

4.   Facial Expressions: Your facial expressions can communicate much about your emotions and interest in the conversation. A smile indicates you're approachable and friendly, while a frown suggests the opposite. Make sure your facial expressions match the tone of the discussion and your body language.

5.   Personal Space Respecting personal space is crucial in communication. Getting too close to someone can be uncomfortable while standing too far away can suggest a lack of interest. Aim for a comfortable distance, usually about an arm's length away.

By keeping these body language dos and don'ts in mind, you can communicate confidently and effectively, leaving a positive and lasting impression on the people you meet.

STRATEGIES FOR MAKING A POSITIVE IMPRESSION

Making a positive impression is crucial for building strong relationships and achieving success personally and professionally. It's not just about smiling and using proper posture. You can use several strategies to make a lasting impression beyond surface-level cues.

1.   Finding Common Ground

Finding common ground with the person you're interacting with can help establish a connection and make them feel more comfortable around you. Look for shared interests or experiences that you can bond over. This can be as simple as asking about their hobbies or finding out where they're from. When you show a genuine interest in what they have to say, you'll create a positive impression.

2.   Being Present in the Moment

Being present now means giving your undivided attention to the person you interact with. Avoid distractions like checking your phone or scanning the room for others to talk to. Listen actively to what the other person is saying and respond thoughtfully. Being fully present will make the other person feel valued and important.

3.   Being Authentic

Being true to yourself is one of the most important strategies for making a positive impression. Don't try to be someone you're not or put on a false persona. People can usually tell when you're not being genuine, and it can damage your credibility and trustworthiness. Instead, be confident in yourself and let your personality shine through. You'll create a more memorable and positive impression when you're authentic.

By incorporating these strategies into your interactions, you can make a lasting impression and build meaningful connections with the people you meet. Remember, it's not just about what you say or how you look – it's about being genuine, present, and finding common ground.

HOW TO DRESS FOR SUCCESS

When it comes to dressing for success, it's essential to remember that different situations call for other attire. Your outfit should not only make you look great but also be appropriate for the occasion. Here are some tips to help you dress for success:

1.   Dress for the occasion: Before choosing an outfit, consider the type of event you'll be attending. A job interview calls for a different dress code than a networking event. If you're unsure what to wear, it's always better to err on caution and dress more formally.

2.   Choose appropriate colors: The colors you wear can also make a difference. Neutral colors like black, gray, and navy blue are always a safe choice, but don't be afraid to add a pop of color to show off your personality. However, avoiding loud, neon colors or busy patterns are essential, as they can be distracting.

3.   Pay attention to fit: The fit of your clothes is also crucial. Ill-fitting clothing can make you look unprofessional and distract you from your message. Ensure your clothes fit properly but are not too tight or loose.

4.   Accessorize strategically: Accessories can be a great way to add personality to your outfit, but be careful not to overdo it. Simple, classic accessories like a watch or a necklace can enhance your outfit without distraction.

5.   Grooming matters: Last but not least, grooming is essential for dressing for success. Ensure your hair is neatly styled, your nails are clean and trimmed, and your shoes are polished. Avoid wearing too much perfume or cologne, as it can be overpowering.

By following these tips, you can choose an outfit that makes you look great and helps you make a positive and professional impression. Dressing for success is about presenting your best self to the world.

THE POWER OF A CONFIDENT HANDSHAKE

A handshake is often the first physical interaction with someone new. It's also one of the most potent ways to make a positive and lasting impression. A weak or timid handshake can leave a negative image and undermine confidence. On the other hand, a firm and a confident handshake can convey strength, warmth, and trustworthiness.

So how do you give a proper handshake? First, make sure your hand is dry and free of any moisture. When you approach the other person, make eye contact and smile warmly. Extend your arm with your palm facing down and your thumb pointing towards the ceiling. Your grip should be firm but not so tight that it's uncomfortable for the other person.

It's important to remember that a handshake isn't just about physical contact. It's also about the nonverbal cues you convey through body language. If you approach the other person with confidence and a genuine smile, they'll be more likely to perceive you as warm and friendly. Conversely, if you come with a stiff or tense body posture, the other person may feel uncomfortable and less inclined to trust you.

In addition to making an excellent first impression, a confident handshake can help establish trust and rapport. Research has shown that a good handshake can release oxytocin, a hormone associated with bonding and trust. A confident handshake can build a stronger connection with the person you're meeting, which can be incredibly valuable in personal and professional settings.

In conclusion, the power of a confident handshake should not be underestimated. It's a simple yet powerful gesture conveying confidence, warmth, and trustworthiness. By mastering the art of the handshake and using it to your advantage, you can make a lasting impression and build strong connections with the people you meet.

You only have one chance to make a first impression, and this chapter has shown how important it is to get it right. By implementing the tips and strategies outlined in this chapter, you can transform your approach to meeting new people and create a positive and lasting impression. From understanding the power of body language to dressing for success, you'll learn how to leave a mark that won't be forgotten. So go ahead, and take the first step towards making a lasting impression - you never know whom you might meet and how it could change your life.

HOW TO READ PEOPLE

Have you ever talked with someone and felt they weren't saying what they meant? Or maybe you've noticed someone's body language indicating they were uncomfortable or anxious but didn't know how to respond appropriately. Reading people is a valuable skill that can help you navigate these situations and become a better communicator.

In this chapter, we'll dive deep into the various aspects of reading people, including body language, facial expressions, tone of voice, and signs of discomfort. By developing these skills, you'll be able to pick up on subtle cues that can give you insight into someone's thoughts and emotions, allowing you to better connect with them and improve your communication. So, let's begin the journey toward becoming a master of reading people.

UNDERSTANDING BODY LANGUAGE

Body language is a crucial component of nonverbal communication that can reveal much about a person's thoughts and emotions. It involves gestures, movements, facial expressions, and posture that can convey meaning and convey messages. Being able to interpret body language can help you better understand those around you and respond more effectively to their needs.

One common body language cue is crossed arms, indicating defensiveness, resistance, or a desire to maintain distance. Fidgeting or tapping can indicate nervousness, restlessness, or anxiety while leaning forward can signal interest, engagement, or enthusiasm. Similarly, leaning back can indicate detachment, disinterest, or a lack of engagement.

Another aspect of body language is eye contact. Direct eye contact can indicate honesty, confidence, or interest while avoiding eye contact can mean discomfort, dishonesty, or anxiety. Blinking rapidly can indicate nervousness, while squinting can show suspicion or skepticism.

The key to understanding body language is to observe a person's overall demeanor and look for patterns and consistencies. It's important to remember that body language cues are not always universal and can vary depending on cultural or individual differences. For example, in some cultures, direct eye contact is considered disrespectful; in others, it's a sign of respect and attentiveness.

By becoming more aware of body language cues and practicing active observation, you can better understand the underlying emotions and attitudes of those around you, leading to more effective communication and stronger relationships.

INTERPRETING FACIAL EXPRESSIONS

Interpreting facial expressions is a crucial aspect of nonverbal communication that can help you better understand the emotional state of the person you're interacting with. It's essential to note that facial expressions vary across cultures, and some expressions may have different meanings in different parts of the world. However, certain universal expressions remain consistent across cultures, such as a smile indicating happiness or a furrowed brow indicating concern.

To interpret facial expressions accurately, you need to pay close attention to the different facial muscles and their movements. Here are some steps to help you solve facial expressions effectively:

1.   Observe the whole face: Start by looking at the entire face, not just a single feature. Different facial features work together to create expressions, so observing the whole face will give you a more accurate understanding of the emotional state.

2.   Look for the most prominent features: Some facial features are more telling than others, such as the eyes, mouth, and eyebrows. These features can give you significant insights into the person's emotional state.

3.   Consider the context: The context of the situation is crucial in interpreting facial expressions. A smile in one situation may indicate happiness, but in another context, it may indicate sarcasm or insincerity.

By following these steps, you can better understand a person's emotional state by interpreting their facial expressions accurately. Practice observing facial expressions and interpreting their meanings in different contexts to improve your nonverbal communication skills.

RECOGNIZING TONE OF VOICE

The tone of voice is another important aspect of communication. It refers to how a person speaks, including style, pitch, and rhythm. The tone of voice can provide essential clues about the speaker's mood and attitude, which can help the listener better understand the message being conveyed. Recognizing tone of voice is a crucial skill for effective communication.

Here are some processes to help you recognize the tone of voice in a conversation:

1.   Listen carefully: The first step to recognizing the tone of voice is to listen carefully. Pay attention to the speaker's tone, pitch, and rhythm. Is their voice high-pitched or low-pitched? Is it fast or slow? Are there any pauses or breaks in their speech? You can better understand the speaker's emotions and attitude by focusing on these details.

2.   Identify the emotions: Once you have listened carefully, try to identify the feelings behind the speaker's tone of voice. Does the tone sound angry, sad, happy, or bored? This can give you essential clues about the speaker's feelings and what they are trying to communicate.

3.   Consider the context: Context is essential regarding the tone of voice. The same technique can mean different things in different situations. For example, a sarcastic tone may be appropriate among friends but not in a professional setting.

Consider the situation and the relationship between you and the speaker when interpreting their style.

4.   Look for nonverbal cues: Nonverbal cues, such as facial expressions and body language, can also provide important clues about the speaker's tone of voice. For example, a person smiling while speaking harshly may use sarcasm or irony.

By recognizing the tone of voice, you can better understand the message and respond appropriately. This skill can be particularly useful in sensitive or complex situations where emotions are involved.

IDENTIFYING SIGNS OF DISCOMFORT

Awareness of the other person's comfort level is essential in any conversation. Sometimes people may not be comfortable sharing their thoughts or emotions, but their body language or tone of voice can reveal their discomfort. By recognizing signs of discomfort, you can adjust your communication approach to help put them at ease and make the conversation more productive.

1.   Body Language: One of the most obvious signs of discomfort is body language. People may cross their arms, lean away, fidget, or avoid eye contact when uncomfortable. Additionally, they may shift their weight from one foot to another or tap their fingers as a sign of nervousness. By noticing these nonverbal cues, you can gauge the other person's comfort level and adjust your communication approach accordingly.

2.   The tone of Voice: Another essential aspect to consider when trying to identify discomfort is the tone of voice. People may use an edgy style or speak softly when uncomfortable or anxious. Alternatively, they may talk rushed or clipped to hurry the conversation. By paying attention to these nuances, you can gain insight into the other person's emotional state and adjust your communication style accordingly.

3.   Verbal Cues: People may also give verbal cues when uncomfortable or anxious. They may repeat themselves or frequently pause in the conversation. Alternatively, they may use language that reflects their discomfort, such as saying, "I'm not sure," or "I'm not comfortable discussing this." By recognizing these cues, you can respond in a way that puts them at ease and keeps the conversation moving forward.

4.   Adjusting Your Approach: Once you've identified signs of discomfort, it's essential to adapt your communication approach to help put the other person at ease. This may involve a gentler tone, offering reassurance, or changing the subject to something more comfortable. The goal is to create a safe and comfy space for others to express themselves and communicate effectively.

Understanding and recognizing signs of discomfort in others can improve your communication skills and build stronger relationships. Whether in personal or professional settings, reading people and responding accordingly is a valuable skill that can help you succeed in all areas of your life.

HOW TO USE THESE SKILLS IN CONVERSATION

Learning to read people is only the first step in becoming a better communicator. To truly use these skills, you need to know how to apply them in conversation. Here are some tips on how to use your newfound skills to improve your communication:

1.   Pay attention to nonverbal cues: Once you have a good grasp of body language, facial expressions, tone of voice, and signs of discomfort, remember these cues during conversations. If someone is crossing their arms or avoiding eye contact, it may indicate that they are feeling uncomfortable or defensive. Adjust your communication style accordingly, perhaps by changing the topic or using more neutral language.

2.   Mirror the other person's body language: Mirroring is adopting similar body language to the person you're speaking with. It can help establish rapport and build trust, making the other person feel more comfortable. For example, if the other person is sitting with their legs crossed, you can cross your legs too. However, be careful not to appear insincere or mimic their every move.

3.   Be aware of your nonverbal cues: Just as paying attention to the other person's nonverbal cues is essential, it's also important to be mindful of your own. Avoid crossing your arms or leaning away from the other person, as this can be seen as defensive or disinterested. Instead, maintain an open posture and make eye contact to signal that you are engaged in the conversation.

4.   Use your observations to guide the conversation: If you notice that the other person seems uncomfortable or hesitant, use your observations to steer the conversation in a different direction. Perhaps they are more comfortable discussing a different topic or need more information before continuing. Using your skills to adapt to the situation ensures the conversation remains productive and positive.

Using these techniques, you can apply your newfound skills in conversation to become a more effective communicator. Remember to be mindful of your nonverbal cues and those of the person you speak with, and adjust your communication style accordingly. With practice, you can become a master at reading people and using that knowledge to build strong relationships and achieve your communication goals.

As humans, we communicate on many levels, not just through words. By mastering the ability to read people, you can gain deeper insight into their thoughts, feelings, and intentions. With these essential skills in your toolkit, you can easily navigate social situations, build stronger relationships, and achieve personal and professional goals. So why not invest your time learning how to read people and unlock a new level of communication?

THE FIVE ELEMENTS OF NON-VERBAL COMMUNICATION

Have you ever wondered why some people seem to have a natural charm and can effortlessly connect with others while others struggle to make a good impression? The secret to their success lies in their ability to master the art of non-verbal communication. Non-verbal communication is a powerful tool that can make or break your ability to communicate with others effectively. In this chapter, we will dive deep into the five essential elements of non-verbal communication, including eye contact, posture, gestures, facial expressions, and tone of voice. You will learn how to use these elements to your advantage and become a master communicator, capable of creating strong connections with others. Get ready to unlock the power of non-verbal communication and take your communication skills to the next level.

EYE CONTACT

Have you ever encountered a conversation where the other person avoids eye contact, leaving you uneasy or unsure of their sincerity? Or maybe you've been in a situation where someone's intense gaze made you uncomfortable or intimidated. Eye contact is a powerful tool in communication, and knowing how to use it effectively can make all the difference in your personal and professional interactions.

Maintaining appropriate eye contact is essential in communication. It shows that you are engaged in the conversation and interested in the speaker's words. It conveys sincerity and trustworthiness and helps establish a connection between the speaker and the listener. When you look someone in the eye, you acknowledge their presence and show them that you value their input.

On the other hand, too much or too little eye contact can be problematic. Avoiding eye contact can indicate boredom, disinterest, or even dishonesty. It can also make the listener feel uncomfortable or uneasy. Conversely, prolonged and intense eye contact can be perceived as aggressive or confrontational, making the speaker uncomfortable.

So, how do you strike the right balance regarding eye contact in communication? Here are some tips:

1.   Make eye contact, but don't stare: Make eye contact with the speaker, but avoid staring. Hold their gaze briefly, then look away to avoid making them uncomfortable.

2.   Match the speaker's eye contact: Try to match the speaker's level of eye contact. If they look at you frequently, reciprocate by looking at them frequently as well.

3.   Be aware of cultural differences: Eye contact norms vary across cultures, so be mindful of what is appropriate in your cultural context.

4.   Use eye contact to convey emotion: Eye contact can express feelings such as interest, empathy, and sincerity. Use it to show the speaker that you are engaged in the conversation and care about what they say.

5.   Don't overthink it: Eye contact should feel natural and comfortable. Don't overthink it or worry too much about how much eye contact you're making. Instead, focus on being present at the moment and actively listening to the speaker.

By mastering the art of eye contact, you can become a more effective communicator and establish meaningful connections with the people you interact with. Remember, maintaining appropriate eye contact is just one element of non-verbal communication, and it works best in combination with other elements such as posture, gestures, facial expressions, and tone of voice.

POSTURE

Posture is one of the key elements of non-verbal communication that can significantly impact how others perceive you. It involves how you hold and positions your body, including your head, shoulders, and spine. Your posture can convey a lot about your level of confidence and authority in a given situation. In this section, we will explore the importance of good posture and how it can be used to improve your communication skills.

Why is Good Posture Important?

Good posture is important for several reasons. Firstly, it can convey a sense of confidence and authority. When you stand or sit up straight with your shoulders back, you look more alert and engaged in the conversation. This can give others the impression that you are confident, knowledgeable, and interested in what they say.

In addition to conveying confidence, good posture can also have a positive impact on your physical health. It can help to prevent back pain, improve breathing, and boost energy levels. When you sit or stand up straight, you are allowing your body to function more efficiently and effectively.

Poor Posture: Conveying a Lack of Confidence

Conversely, poor posture can convey a lack of confidence and interest in the conversation. Slouching or hunching over can make you appear disinterested or unengaged in what is being discussed. It can also give others the impression that you lack confidence or authority.

In addition to the negative impact on your communication skills, poor posture can also negatively affect your physical health. It can lead to back pain, fatigue, and breathing difficulties.

How to Improve Your Posture

Improving your posture is relatively simple and can significantly impact your communication skills. Start by becoming aware of how you hold your body to improve your posture. Sit or stand up straight with your shoulders back and your head high. Avoid slouching or hunching over, and try to keep your spine straight.

Developing good posture habits may take some time, but it will become easier and more natural with practice. Try yoga or Pilates to improve your posture and strengthen your core muscles.

Posture is an important element of non-verbal communication that can significantly impact how others perceive you. Good posture conveys confidence and authority, while poor posture can convey a lack of interest and enthusiasm. By becoming aware of your posture and working to improve it, you can become a more effective communicator and present yourself with greater confidence and authority.

GESTURES

Gestures are one of the most powerful and versatile elements of non-verbal communication. They are not just limited to hand movements but can also involve the direction of the head, face, and other body parts. Gestures are essential to communication, as they convey different emotions, attitudes, and ideas.

There are many types of gestures, each with its meaning and significance. For example, when we want to emphasize a point or show excitement, we may use large, expansive gestures such as raising our arms or jumping up and down. Conversely, we may use smaller, more subtle gestures such as fidgeting or tapping fingers when expressing doubt or hesitation.

However, it's important to use gestures appropriately and in moderation. Overusing gestures can be distracting and take away from the message we are trying to convey. Similarly, using inappropriate gestures can lead to misinterpretation or offend others. Therefore, it is crucial to be mindful of our gestures and use them intentionally.

One effective way to use gestures is to synchronize them with our words. For example, when we want to emphasize a point, we can use gestures that match our message, such as raising our hand when saying "stop." This synchronization can help to reinforce our message and make it more memorable.

In addition, we can also use gestures to build rapport and connect with others. For example, mirroring someone's gestures can help to establish a sense of trust and understanding. Similarly, using open, welcoming gestures such as a smile or nod can help to create a positive and welcoming atmosphere.

Gestures are a powerful tool for effective communication, but using them in moderation and with intention is important. By being mindful of our gestures and using them to reinforce our message and build rapport, we can become more confident and effective communicators.

FACIAL EXPRESSIONS

Facial expressions are an essential element of non-verbal communication. They can convey emotions and provide valuable insight into a person's thoughts and feelings. Facial expressions can also emphasize or complement spoken words, making them a powerful tool for effective communication.

To understand the significance of facial expressions, it's essential to recognize their key emotions. The most common sentiments expressed through facial expressions include happiness, surprise, anger, disgust, and sadness. Recognizing these emotions in others and appropriately responding to them can be a valuable asset in any personal or professional setting.

It's essential to use facial expressions in an authentic way that matches the tone of the conversation. For example, a smile may not be appropriate if someone is expressing a sense of sadness. However, showing empathy and concern with a gentle frown or concerned look can communicate your understanding and support.

Facial expressions can also be used to regulate communication, either by emphasizing the intended message or by providing subtle cues to the speaker's inner thoughts. For example, a raised eyebrow can signify disbelief or skepticism, while a nod of agreement can indicate that the listener is engaged and understands the speaker's message.

Facial expressions are a crucial component of non-verbal communication. They can convey various emotions, regulate communication, and complement spoken words. By mastering facial expressions, you can become a more effective communicator, build better relationships, and significantly impact your personal and professional life.

TONE OF VOICE

The tone of voice is a powerful tool in communication that can influence how others receive our message. It's not just about what we say but how we say it that matters. A monotone voice can make the listener feel bored or uninterested, while an enthusiastic tone can convey excitement and energy.

When we communicate with others, our tone of voice can be influenced by many factors, such as our mood, personality, cultural background, and the context of the situation. For example, a job interview may require a more formal and professional tone, while a casual conversation with friends may call for a more relaxed and informal style.

It's important to know our tone of voice and how others perceive it. A harsh or condescending tone can make the listener feel defensive or disrespected, while a calm and reassuring manner can create a sense of trust and comfort. We can adjust our voice style to the situation and better connect with our audience by paying attention to our voice style.

One way to improve our tone of voice is to practice active listening. When we actively listen to others, we can pick up on the emotions and style of their message and respond appropriately.

We can also pay attention to our tone of voice by recording ourselves speaking or asking for feedback from others.

In addition, using vocal inflections can also enhance our tone of voice. Vocal inflections involve changing our voice's voice's pitch, and volume, an This can make our message more engaging and interesting to the listener.

Overall, being mindful of our tone of voice is essential By using an appropriate tone, we can convey our message more impactfully and connect better with our audience.

Communication is not just about the words we speak but also about the non-verbal cues we give off. By understanding and mastering the five elements of non-verbal communication, you can become a more confident and effective communicator in any situation. So, whether you're giving a presentation, conversing with a colleague, or simply trying to make a good impression, incorporating these techniques into your communication style can help you convey your message with greater impact and achieve the desired results.

DIFFERENT PEOPLE, DIFFERENT APPROACH

Effective communication is not just about the words you say. It's also about understanding whom you're communicating with and adjusting your communication style accordingly. Whether you're communicating with coworkers, clients, friends, or family members, tailoring your approach can make all the difference in the conversation's outcome.

In this chapter, we'll explore the importance of tailoring your communication style and how it can lead to better outcomes in both personal and professional settings. We'll examine how different personality types can affect communication and provide strategies for adapting your approach to fit different personality types. We'll also discuss the importance of cultural differences in touch and provide tips for connecting with people from different backgrounds. Finally, we'll delve into techniques for building rapport and explain how this skill can help you establish deeper connections with others. By the end of this chapter, you'll have a toolkit of strategies and techniques for tailoring your communication style to connect with anyone, anywhere.

TAILORING YOUR COMMUNICATION STYLE

There are a few key considerations when tailoring your communication style. First, it's important to understand the individual's personality type. Different personality types may respond better to different communication styles, so it's helpful to understand personality types such as introverts, extroverts, analytical thinkers, and intuitive thinkers. By identifying the individual's personality type, you can adjust your communication style to make them more receptive to your message.

Another important factor to consider is cultural differences. Different cultures may have different communication norms and expectations, so it's important to be aware of these differences and adjust your communication style accordingly. For example, some cultures value direct and assertive communication, while others value indirect and respectful communication. By taking the time to understand and respect these cultural differences, you can avoid misunderstandings and build stronger relationships.

Finally, building rapport is an essential part of tailoring your communication style. By connecting with the individual on a personal level, you can establish trust and create a more comfortable and productive environment for communication. This can involve finding common ground, asking open-ended questions, and actively listening to their responses. By building rapport, you can make a foundation for effective communication and stronger relationships with those around you.

UNDERSTANDING DIFFERENT PERSONALITY TYPES

Understanding different personality types is an important aspect of effective communication. It's easy to fall into the trap of assuming that everyone communicates in the same way. However, the reality is that we all have unique personalities that impact the way we interact with others. By taking the time to understand different personality types, you can tailor your communication style to suit the needs of the individual you're communicating with. This can significantly affect how your message is received and how effectively you can connect with others.

One common approach to understanding personality types is the Myers-Briggs Type Indicator (MBTI), which classifies people into one of 16 personality types based on their preferences for different ways of thinking and acting. Every 16 types have unique strengths and weaknesses and respond best to specific communication styles. For example, someone with an extroverted personality type may enjoy a more lively and energetic conversation, while someone with an introverted personality may prefer a quieter and more thoughtful discussion. Understanding these preferences and adapting your communication style accordingly can create a more comfortable and effective communication experience.

Another approach to understanding personality types is the Big Five Personality Traits model, which categorizes people based on their openness, conscientiousness, extraversion, agreeableness, and neuroticism levels. These personality traits can give you insight into the best communication styles for different individuals. For example, someone who scores high in extraversion may prefer a more social and interactive conversation. In contrast, someone who scores high in neuroticism may prefer a more calm and reassuring approach. By understanding and adapting to these different personality traits, you can create an effective and comfortable communication style for everyone involved.

In summary, understanding different personality types is crucial for effective communication. Whether you're using the MBTI or the Big Five Personality Traits model, taking the time to understand and adapt to different personality types can significantly affect how your message is received and how effectively you can connect with others.

ADJUSTING TO CULTURAL DIFFERENCES

Adjusting to cultural differences is essential to effective communication, especially in today's diverse world. Culture influences communication styles and how people interpret messages, making it crucial to be aware of and respect cultural differences. It's not just about being polite or politically correct; it's about building relationships and connecting with people from different cultures.

To communicate effectively across cultures, it's necessary to understand the differences in communication styles, body language, and non-verbal cues. For example, some cultures value direct and assertive communication, while others prioritize indirect and polite communication. In some cultures, maintaining eye contact is a sign of respect and attentiveness; in others, it may be considered rude or confrontational. These differences can impact how your message is received and understood, making it important to adjust your communication style accordingly.

One key to adjusting to cultural differences is to be open-minded and curious about other cultures. This means asking questions, actively listening, and showing interest in different perspectives. By doing so, you'll not only improve your communication skills but also broaden your cultural knowledge and understanding. In this chapter, we'll explore various cultural communication styles and provide tips on adjusting your communication style to connect more effectively with people from different cultures. We'll also discuss avoiding common cultural misunderstandings and navigating potentially sensitive topics.

HOW TO CONNECT WITH PEOPLE FROM DIFFERENT BACKGROUNDS

Connecting with people from different backgrounds can be a rewarding experience that broadens your understanding of the world but can also be challenging. Communicating effectively with people from different backgrounds requires an open-minded approach and a willingness to learn and understand different perspectives. In this section, we'll explore techniques for building rapport with individuals from diverse backgrounds and how to navigate cultural differences in communication.

One of the key strategies for connecting with people from different backgrounds is active listening. This involves giving your full attention to the person speaking, acknowledging their perspective, and asking questions to understand their thoughts and feelings better. Active listening shows that you value the person and their ideas and can also help you find common ground.

Another way to connect with people from different backgrounds is to find common ground. This can be simple: a shared interest in sports, music, or movies. When you find common ground with someone, it can help break down barriers and create a connection. It's important to remember that even if you don't share the same cultural background or experiences, you can still find common ground with someone based on shared values, beliefs, or interests.

Acknowledging and respecting cultural differences is also crucial when communicating with people from different backgrounds. This means being aware of cultural norms, values, and traditions and avoiding assumptions or stereotypes. Respect for someone's culture and beliefs demonstrates that you value and appreciate their unique perspective. It's also important to be aware of nonverbal communication and body language, as these can differ across cultures.

By utilizing these techniques and approaching communication with an open mind and a willingness to learn, you can build strong relationships with people from different backgrounds and broaden your understanding of the world.

TECHNIQUES FOR BUILDING RAPPORT

Building rapport is an important skill to master for effective communication. By creating a connection with your audience, you can foster an environment of trust and respect that will help you achieve your communication goals. You can use several techniques to build rapport, and we'll explore them in this section.

One technique for building rapport is to mirror the body language of the person you're communicating with. This means copying their posture, gestures, and facial expressions. Mirroring can help create a sense of familiarity and comfort, making the other person more receptive to your message. It's important to be subtle and natural when mirroring, as overdoing it can be insincere or creepy.

Another effective technique for building rapport is active listening. This means fully focusing on the person you're communicating with and showing that you understand and value their perspective. It involves making eye contact, nodding, and asking clarifying questions. Active listening shows that you care about what the other person has to say and can help you gain their trust.

Finding common ground is a powerful way to build rapport. When you discover shared interests or experiences, it creates a bond between you and the other person. Look for ways to connect personally, such as discussing hobbies, family, or work experiences. Finding common ground will create a sense of camaraderie that can help break down barriers and build trust.

Effective communication is not just about delivering your message; it's also about connecting with your audience in a way that resonates with them. Understanding that different people require different approaches allows you to adapt your communication style to achieve your desired outcome. Whether you're dealing with a colleague, a friend, or a client, learning how to tailor your communication style is a powerful tool that can lead to successful outcomes in both personal and professional situations.

In this chapter, we've explored techniques for building rapport and connecting with people from different backgrounds. From mirroring body language to active listening, these techniques can help you build trust and establish a strong foundation for successful communication. By taking the time to understand different personality types and adjusting to cultural differences, you can also create a more inclusive and welcoming environment that encourages open and honest communication.

THE POWER OF EMPATHY

Humans are wired to connect with others and understand their perspectives. Empathy is the ability to put yourself in someone else's shoes and feel what they feel. It's critical to effective communication and can help you build trust and deepen relationships. In this chapter, we will delve into the power of empathy and how it can transform your communication skills.

We'll discuss empathy and how it differs from sympathy or pity. Then, we'll explore practical ways to develop and apply your empathy skills in your personal and professional life. We'll examine the benefits of empathy, including increased understanding and improved emotional intelligence. Additionally, we'll look at how to show empathy in conversation by using active listening, reflecting on feelings, and asking open-ended questions. Finally, we'll explore the role of the heart in conflict resolution and how it can help you navigate difficult conversations with grace and understanding.

WHAT IS EMPATHY?

Empathy is a complex human ability that allows individuals to connect with others on a deeper level by understanding and sharing their emotions. It involves not only recognizing and identifying emotions in others but also experiencing them vicariously. This shared experience of emotions enables people to connect and establish deeper relationships with one another.

Empathy can manifest in different ways, including cognitive empathy and emotional empathy. Cognitive empathy refers to the ability to understand and comprehend someone else's perspective, thoughts, and feelings. On the other hand, the vibrant heart involves experiencing the same emotions as another person. This empathy enables individuals to resonate with others and show genuine care and concern for their well-being.

Empathy is an important skill that enables people to interact with one another more effectively, leading to better communication, stronger relationships, and increased well-being. It can help individuals understand others' perspectives, identify with their emotions, and respond appropriately. Empathy is beneficial for personal relationships and professional ones, including customer service, leadership, and teamwork.

DEVELOPING EMPATHY

Developing empathy is a process that requires intentional effort and practice. Here are some steps you can take to build your empathy skills:

1.   Active Listening: Active listening involves focusing on the speaker and fully absorbing their message. To actively listen, avoid distractions, and maintain eye contact with the speaker. Use verbal cues such as nodding or saying "mm-hmm" to show that you are listening. Repeat what the speaker said to ensure you understand their message correctly.

2.   Perspective-Taking: Perspective-taking is the ability to see a situation from someone else's point of view. To practice perspective-taking, try to put yourself in the other person's shoes and imagine their feelings. Ask yourself what you would do if you were in their situation. This can help you understand their perspective and respond with empathy.

3.   Non-Verbal Cues: Respond to non-verbal cues such as body language and facial expressions. These cues can provide valuable insights into how someone feels, even if they are not verbally expressing it. For example, crossed arms may indicate defensiveness or discomfort, while a smile may indicate happiness or contentment.

4.   Validation: Validating someone's feelings can show that you understand and empathize with them. To validate someone, acknowledge their feelings and tell them you hear them. For example, you might say, "I can understand why you feel that way," or "That must have been difficult for you."

Practicing these skills allows you to develop empathy and become a more effective communicator.

THE BENEFITS OF EMPATHY

Empathy is a powerful tool that can positively impact both the giver and the receiver. Here are some of the benefits of empathy:

1.   Builds trust: When you show empathy towards others, they are likelier to trust and open up to you. Kindness creates a safe space where people feel heard and understood.

2.   Improves communication: Empathy helps break down communication barriers by fostering a deeper understanding of others. This understanding can help to create more meaningful and effective communication.

3.   Enhances relationships: Empathy is key to building strong and healthy relationships. When people feel understood and validated, they are more likely to form deep and lasting connections.

4.   Promotes personal growth: Practicing empathy can help you develop a deeper understanding of your own emotions and the emotions of others. This can lead to personal growth and a better understanding of the world around you.

5.   Reduces stress: When people feel understood and supported, they are less likely to feel stressed or overwhelmed. Empathy can help to reduce stress levels and promote overall well-being.

Empathy has numerous benefits that can enhance our relationships, communication, and personal growth. By practicing empathy, we can create a more positive and compassionate world.

HOW TO SHOW EMPATHY IN CONVERSATION

Empathy is a vital component of effective communication, and it's essential to show it in conversations. When you show empathy, you acknowledge and understand the other person's feelings, thoughts, and perspectives. In this section, we'll delve deeper into specific techniques and behaviors that you can use to show empathy in conversation.

One effective way to show empathy is acknowledging the other person's feelings. You can do this by using phrases such as "I can see that you're upset" or "That sounds frustrating." This shows you're paying attention to their emotions and caring about their well-being.

Using open-ended questions is another effective way to show empathy in conversation. These questions encourage the other person to share more information and feelings. For example, instead of asking, "Did you have a good day?" you can ask, "What was your day like?" This shows that you're interested in hearing more about their experience, allowing them to express themselves fully.

Reflecting on what you've heard is another useful technique for showing empathy. This involves summarizing what the other person has said to you to confirm that you understand them correctly. For example, you might say, "So, what I'm hearing is that you're feeling frustrated because of the lack of communication from your team?" This demonstrates that you're actively listening and trying to understand their perspective.

Finally, it's crucial to be aware of your tone of voice and body language when showing empathy. A warm, caring tone of voice can go a long way in demonstrating empathy, while crossed arms or a defensive posture can convey the opposite. By being mindful of your non-verbal cues, you can show that you're fully present and engaged in the conversation.

THE ROLE OF EMPATHY IN CONFLICT RESOLUTION

Empathy is a powerful tool in conflict resolution that can help create a peaceful resolution. When we conflict with someone, focusing is natural. However, by practicing empathy, we can shift our focus to understanding the other person's point of view, emotions, and needs. This shift in perspective can help us connect with the other person on a deeper level, leading to a more constructive and positive resolution.

One of the benefits of empathy in conflict resolution is that it can help to de-escalate the situation. When we feel like we're being heard and understood, we're more likely to lower our guard and become more receptive to the other person's point of view. This can help to reduce the tension in the situation and create a more cooperative environment for communication.

Empathy also helps to build trust in the relationship, which is essential for a successful resolution. When we show empathy towards the other person, we care about their perspective and emotions. This can create a safe space for communication, which can help to facilitate a mutually acceptable solution.

Empathy plays a critical role in conflict resolution by helping people to understand each other's perspectives, de-escalate tense situations, build trust, and find mutually acceptable solutions.

Practicing empathy can create a more peaceful and positive outcome for everyone involved.

Empathy has become more important than ever in today's fast-paced and often disconnected world. By developing your empathy skills, you can create deeper connections with those around you and cultivate a sense of understanding and compassion. Whether you're communicating with a friend, a family member, a colleague, or even a stranger, empathy can help you to understand their perspective better and build trust in your relationships. Moreover, practicing empathy can help you to develop a greater sense of self-awareness and emotional intelligence, which can positively impact other areas of your life, such as personal growth and career success.

In this chapter, we've explored the concept of empathy and how it can benefit you as a communicator and a human being. We've discussed the importance of developing empathy skills, how to show empathy in conversation, and the critical role of empathy in conflict resolution. By taking the time to cultivate empathy in your life, you can become a more effective and compassionate communicator and create more meaningful connections with those around you. Remember, empathy is not just a tool for communication but a mindset and a way of being that can transform your relationships and your life.

THE SEARCH FOR SIMILARITY

Effective communication often hinges on finding common ground with the people we interact with. The similarity search can help us connect, build rapport, and establish trust. This chapter will explore the concept of finding common ground, the benefits of similarity, and techniques for uncovering shared interests and experiences. We'll also discuss using these commonalities to build rapport and strengthen relationships.

FINDING COMMON GROUND

When we interact with others, it can be easy to focus on our differences and overlook our commonalities. However, finding common ground can be a powerful way to break down barriers and build connections. When we realize that we share common interests, values, or experiences, we're more likely to feel a sense of kinship and rapport with others.

One of the benefits of finding common ground is that it can help to reduce tension and create a more positive atmosphere. When we feel that we have something in common with someone, we're less likely to be defensive or guarded in our interactions. This can lead to more open and honest communication and a greater sense of trust and mutual understanding.

To find common ground, listening to others and looking for opportunities to connect actively is important. This can involve asking open-ended questions, sharing personal experiences, and seeking out shared interests. By doing so, you can uncover areas of overlap and build a foundation for stronger relationships. In the following sections, we'll explore techniques for finding commonalities and using them to build rapport and connect with others.

THE BENEFITS OF SIMILARITY

Research has shown that finding similarities can benefit communication and relationships. When we share commonalities with others, we tend to feel more at ease with them and are more likely to bond over shared interests and experiences. The following are some of the key benefits of finding common ground:

1.   Increased Trust: When we find similarities with someone, we trust them more. This is because we assume that people who share our values and beliefs are likelier, honest, and reliable.

2.   Greater Cooperation: People who share common goals and interests are more likely to cooperate to achieve those goals. When we feel a sense of camaraderie with someone, we're more willing to work together towards a common objective.

3.   Improved Communication: Finding similarities with someone can improve communication by creating a shared language and understanding. When we have common ground with someone, we're more likely to be on the same page and able to communicate effectively.

4.   Stronger Relationships: People who share similarities tend to have stronger and more fulfilling relationships. When we feel

connected with someone, we're more likely to invest time and effort into building and maintaining that relationship.

By understanding the benefits of similarity, we can consciously find common ground with others and improve our communication and relationships.

TECHNIQUES FOR FINDING COMMONALITIES

One of the most effective ways to connect is to find commonalities or shared interests. However, this can be easier said than done, especially when interacting with people you don't know well or who have different backgrounds or interests than you do. Fortunately, there are several techniques you can use to uncover shared interests and experiences, including:

1.   Active listening: One of the best ways to find common ground with someone is to actively listen to what they're saying. This means paying close attention to their words, tone of voice, and body language and asking clarifying questions to show that you're interested in what they have to say.

2.   Asking open-ended questions: Open-ended questions can't be answered with a simple "yes" or "no." They encourage the person to share more about themselves and can help you discover shared interests or experiences. For example, instead of asking, "Do you like sports?" you could ask, "What sports do you enjoy playing or watching?"

3.   Finding commonalities in experiences and values: Even if you don't share the same hobbies or interests as someone else,

you may still have shared experiences or values that you can bond over. For example, if you both grew up in the same city or have a passion for helping others, you can use these shared experiences or values as a starting point for building rapport.

4.   Paying attention to nonverbal cues: Nonverbal cues, such as facial expressions and body language, can also provide clues about shared interests or experiences. For example, if someone is wearing a shirt with a band you like, you can use this to start a conversation about music.

By using these techniques, you can more easily find common ground with others, which can help you build stronger relationships and improve your communication skills.

USING COMMON INTERESTS TO BUILD RAPPORT

Starting a conversation with someone can sometimes feel daunting, but finding common interests can make it easier. By talking about shared hobbies or interests, you can immediately create a connection and show that you have something in common. This can help put the other person at ease and make them more receptive to what you say.

Once you've established common interests, using them to build rapport is important. For example, you could suggest walking together if you both enjoy hiking. This not only provides an opportunity to do something fun together but also helps to solidify your shared interest. Additionally, sharing an experience can create lasting memories and further strengthen your relationship.

Another technique for building rapport through common interests is actively listening and showing genuine interest in the other person's hobbies or passions. Ask questions and try to learn more about what they enjoy. Not only does this demonstrate that you care about their interests, but it also allows you to learn something new and potentially discover new shared interests.

Overall, using common interests to build rapport effectively strengthens relationships and creates a positive and enjoyable communication experience.

THE POWER OF SHARED EXPERIENCES

Shared experiences can create a deep sense of connection and community among individuals, no matter how different they may seem on the surface. Whether reminiscing about past experiences, sharing stories, or participating in group activities, shared experiences can forge bonds that transcend differences. In this section, we'll dive deeper into the power of shared experiences and how they can be used to build connections with others.

Reminiscing about past experiences is a common way to bond with others. It's a powerful tool for creating a shared history and reminding people of their good times together. Sharing stories and memories can also help build empathy and understanding, allowing individuals to see things from each other's perspectives.

Additionally, group activities such as team-building exercises or volunteering can be a great way to create shared experiences and build connections. When people work towards a common goal, they often form a sense of camaraderie and unity.

The power of shared experiences goes beyond just building connections - it can also have significant benefits for mental health and well-being. Research has shown that people who participate in shared experiences report higher happiness and life satisfaction levels. Shared experiences can also help reduce stress and anxiety, providing a sense of belonging and social support. By actively seeking out and participating in shared experiences, individuals can build stronger connections with others and improve their mental and emotional health.

Connecting with others through shared interests and experiences is a surefire way to improve communication skills and build lasting relationships. By discovering common ground and using it as a foundation, we can create deeper understanding and empathy with others. Through this chapter, we've learned about the benefits of similarity, the various techniques for finding commonalities, and the power of shared experiences in building strong connections.

As we've seen, reminiscing, sharing stories, and participating in group activities are just a few examples of how shared experiences can bring people together. We can create lasting memories and meaningful relationships by tapping into these powerful bonding agents. Whether participating in a hobby, volunteering for a cause, or simply sharing a common interest, finding common ground is essential to effective communication and a key factor in building strong connections with others.

SECRET TO ASKING QUESTIONS

Asking questions is an essential skill that can help us better understand the world around its people and us. Through questioning, we can gain insight into other people's perspectives, learn new information, and deepen our connections with others. We can facilitate communication, build trust, and establish a solid foundation for relationships by asking the right questions.

However, not all questions are created equal. How we ask questions can significantly impact the responses we receive and the outcomes of our interactions. By learning how to ask open-ended questions, we can encourage others to share more information and insights, leading to a deeper understanding of their thoughts and feelings. Probing questions, on the other hand, can help us to uncover hidden motives and clarify points of confusion. By mastering the art of asking questions, we can become more effective communicators and build stronger relationships.

TYPES OF QUESTIONS

We can use several types of questions to elicit specific types of responses from the person we are communicating with. Closed-ended questions, for example, can be answered with a simple "yes" or "no" response. These questions are useful when we need to gather specific information quickly, but they can also limit the conversation and prevent deeper exploration of a topic. On the other hand, open-ended questions encourage longer and more detailed responses, allowing for a more in-depth discussion. These questions are useful for building rapport and understanding someone's perspective or feelings.

Probing or follow-up questions are designed to dig deeper into a specific topic. These questions can be used to gather more information, clarify a point, or challenge someone's assumptions. Probing questions are particularly useful in professional settings, such as interviews or meetings, as it can help uncover important details and ensure everyone is on the same page.

In addition to these types of questions, there are also leading questions designed to steer the conversation in a particular direction. These questions can be useful in negotiations or when trying to persuade someone, but they can also be manipulative and damage the trust in a conversation. Using leading questions carefully and considering the other person's perspective is important.

HOW TO ASK OPEN-ENDED QUESTIONS

1.   Understanding the importance of open-ended questions

Asking open-ended questions can help create a safe communication space and encourage the other person to share their thoughts and feelings. It can also help to facilitate a deeper understanding of the person and their perspectives. When we ask open-ended questions, we show that we're genuinely interested in what the other person has to say and are willing to listen.

2.   Crafting open-ended questions

Crafting open-ended questions requires a bit of thought and consideration. These questions encourage the other person to elaborate on their response rather than just giving a one-word answer. They typically start with words like "What," "Why," and "How." For example, "What are your thoughts on the current political climate?" or "How do you feel about the recent changes at work?"

3.   Using open-ended questions effectively

Using open-ended questions effectively involves actively listening to the other person's response and using their answer as a springboard for further discussion. It's important to avoid interrupting or leading the conversation in a particular direction. Instead, allow the conversation to flow naturally, and ask follow-up questions based on the other person's response.

Overall, asking open-ended questions is valuable for building relationships and establishing connections with others. By understanding the importance of open-ended questions, crafting them thoughtfully, and using them effectively, we can engage in more meaningful conversations and deepen our understanding of those around us.

STRATEGIES FOR ASKING PROBING QUESTIONS

There are several strategies you can use to ask probing questions effectively. Here are some of the key processes:

1.   Clarifying questions: When someone shares information with you, explaining what they mean is important. Ask questions

to gain a better understanding of what they're saying. Clarifying questions can help you avoid misunderstandings and ensure you're on the same page.

2.   Reflective questions: These types of questions help the other person to reflect on their thoughts, feelings, and experiences. Thoughtful questions can be used to encourage someone to think more deeply about a situation or to explore their own beliefs and values.

3.   Hypothetical questions: Hypothetical questions can be used to explore alternative scenarios or to get someone to think about a situation from a different perspective. They can help to open up a conversation and generate new ideas.

4.   Challenging questions: Challenging questions can be useful when challenging someone's assumptions or beliefs. They can be used to encourage someone to think critically about their position and to explore alternative viewpoints.

It's important to use probing questions carefully and sensitively, as they can sometimes be perceived as intrusive or confrontational. Try to use them in a way that shows genuine interest and concern for the other person's perspective.

HOW TO USE QUESTIONS TO BUILD RAPPORT

There are several key processes to remember when using questions to build rapport.

1.   Active listening: One of the most important aspects of building rapport through questioning is active listening. It's essential to pay attention to what the other person is saying and respond appropriately. This includes verbal and nonverbal cues, such as body language and tone of voice. By showing that you are actively engaged in the conversation, the other person will feel valued and respected, which can help to build trust and create a positive connection.

2.   Showing interest: Another critical aspect of using questions to build rapport is showing genuine interest in the other person. Ask open-ended questions that invite the other person to share more about themselves. Avoid closed-ended questions that only require a simple yes or no answer. By asking open-ended questions, you demonstrate that you're interested in getting to know them better and can help to facilitate a deeper connection.

3.   Finding common ground: Finding common interests or experiences is an effective way to build rapport quickly. Ask questions that help you discover shared interests or experiences, such as hobbies, favorite movies, or travel destinations. When you find common ground, you create a bond that can help to establish a positive connection and foster a deeper relationship.

Following these processes, you can use questions to build rapport and establish connections with others. Building rapport through questioning is a powerful tool for personal and professional relationships. When used effectively, it can help to improve communication, build trust, and create a positive and lasting connection.

NOW SHUT UP AND LISTEN!

Communication is a two-way street, and listening is as essential as speaking. Yet, many of us struggle with listening effectively, whether distracted by our thoughts or eager to interject our opinions. In this chapter, we'll delve into the crucial role that hearing plays in communication and relationships. By exploring active listening techniques, understanding the benefits of reflective listening, and discovering how to show others that we're truly engaged, we can become more skilled listeners and ultimately strengthen our connections. So, let's learn how to tune in and truly listen.

THE IMPORTANCE OF LISTENING

The importance of listening cannot be overstated regarding effective communication. Listening is a key part of building relationships and understanding the needs and perspectives of others. It is not just about hearing what the other person is saying but also about being present and attentive to their words and emotions.

Listening is a sign of respect and shows that you value the other person's thoughts and opinions. Listening actively lets you gain insight into their perspective and understand their needs and expectations. This can help you build trust and establish rapport, essential to effective communication.

Effective listening also involves being able to read and interpret nonverbal cues such as facial expressions, body language, and tone of voice. This can help you to understand the speaker's emotions and gain a deeper understanding of their message. It also enables you to respond appropriately, whether that means offering support, reassurance, or constructive feedback.

In contrast, failing to listen can have serious consequences for communication and relationships. Interrupting or ignoring the speaker can cause frustration, resentment, and damage to the relationship. It can also lead to misunderstandings and misinterpretations, which can cause further conflict and communication breakdown.

Overall, the importance of listening cannot be underestimated in effective communication. It is essential for building relationships, gaining understanding, and responding appropriately to others. By listening actively, we can enhance our communication skills and build stronger, more meaningful relationships with those around us.

ACTIVE LISTENING TECHNIQUES

Active listening is a critical skill that is essential for effective communication. It involves giving the speaker your undivided attention and showing them you are fully present and engaged in the conversation. Active listening helps you better understand the speaker's message, build stronger relationships, and avoid misunderstandings. In this section, we'll discuss some active listening techniques to help you become a better listener and improve your communication skills.

1.   Pay Attention: One of the most important aspects of active listening is paying attention to the speaker. This means focusing on what they are saying and blocking out any distractions. Pay attention to the speaker's tone of voice, body language, and the context of the conversation. This will help you better understand their message.

2.   Ask Clarifying Questions: Asking clarifying questions can help you better understand the speaker's message. It shows that you are interested in what they say and want to ensure you fully understand their point. Clarifying questions include "Can you explain that in more detail?" or "Can you give me an example of what you mean?"

3.   Paraphrase: Paraphrasing is restating the speaker's message in your own words. This technique shows that you are actively listening and helps ensure you understand the speaker's message correctly. For example, you could say, "So, what I hear you saying is..." or "In other words, you mean..."

4.   Summarize: Summarizing involves concisely restating the speaker's message. This technique can help ensure that you have understood the main points of the conversation and can help the speaker feel heard and understood. For example, you could say, "So, if I understand correctly, you're saying that..." or "In summary, the main point is..."

5.   Provide Feedback: Feedback involves giving the speaker a response demonstrating that you have understood their message. This could include nodding your head, maintaining eye contact,

or using verbal cues such as "I see" or "I understand." Feedback can help the speaker feel heard and understood, improving the conversation's quality.

Active listening is a crucial skill for effective communication. By paying attention, asking clarifying questions, paraphrasing, summarizing, and providing feedback, you can become a better listener and build stronger relationships with those around you.

HOW TO AVOID INTERRUPTING

Interrupting someone during a conversation can be a common communication barrier and hinder effective communication. Interrupting can indicate a lack of respect, show disinterest, or even suggest that the interrupter believes they have the right to control the conversation. It can also cause the speaker to lose their train of thought, resulting in both parties' frustration. Therefore, learning how to avoid interrupting during a conversation is essential.

One way to avoid interrupting is to practice active listening. Active listening involves focusing on the speaker and their message instead of thinking about your response or waiting for your turn to talk. Being present in the conversation allows you to listen more effectively and reduce the urge to interrupt. Additionally, asking open-ended questions or paraphrasing what the speaker said can demonstrate that you are actively listening and encourage the speaker to continue.

Another way to avoid interrupting is to practice patience. Sometimes we interrupt because the conversation is moving too slowly or the speaker is not getting to the point quickly enough. However, it is important to remember that everyone communicates at their own pace and that conversations take time. By practicing patience and allowing the speaker to express themselves fully, you can avoid interrupting and show that you respect their thoughts and ideas.

It is also essential to be aware of your communication style and tendencies. If you find that you interrupt frequently, take some time to reflect on why that may be. Are you anxious about getting your point across? Are you more interested in being heard than in listening to others? By understanding your communication style, you can change it and become a better listener.

In conclusion, interrupting can hinder effective communication and damage relationships. By practicing active listening, patience, and self-awareness, we can learn to avoid interrupting conversations and become better listeners.

THE BENEFITS OF REFLECTIVE LISTENING

The benefits of reflective listening cannot be overstated regarding effective communication. Reflective listening involves paraphrasing or summarizing the speaker's message to ensure understanding and demonstrate that you are actively listening. It allows the listener to understand the speaker's message better and provides a sense of validation for the speaker. In this section, we'll discuss the benefits of reflective listening in detail.

1.   Encourages Openness and Trust Reflective listening can create a safe and comfortable environment for communication, which can lead to more honest and open communication. It shows that the listener is actively engaged and interested in the speaker's words. When the speaker feels listened to and understood, it can build trust and encourage them to share more.

2.   Resolves Misunderstandings Reflective listening helps the listener to clarify any misunderstandings that may arise during a conversation. By summarizing or paraphrasing the speaker's message, the listener can ensure they understand the news accurately. If there are any misunderstandings, they can be addressed and resolved immediately.

3.   Demonstrates Empathy Reflective listening is a powerful tool to demonstrate empathy towards the speaker. When the listener reflects on the speaker's message, it shows that they understand the speaker's feelings and point of view. It can help the speaker feel validated and heard.

4.   Improves Relationships Reflective listening can improve relationships by creating a deeper understanding and connection between the listener and the speaker. It shows that the listener values the speaker's thoughts and feelings, which can help to build stronger relationships.

In conclusion, the benefits of reflective listening are significant and can greatly improve communication and relationships. By actively listening and reflecting on the speaker's message, the listener can create a safe and comfortable environment for communication, resolve misunderstandings, demonstrate empathy, and improve relationships.

HOW TO SHOW YOU'RE LISTENING WITHOUT INTERRUPTING

A crucial aspect of effective communication is showing that you are listening without interrupting. Interrupting someone while speaking can be perceived as disrespectful and cause the speaker to feel ignored or undervalued. Fortunately, there are several ways to show that you are listening without interrupting.

First, it's important to maintain eye contact with the speaker. This demonstrates that you are fully engaged in the conversation and actively listening to what they are saying. It also helps to avoid distractions, such as looking at your phone or glancing around the room, which can give the impression that you are not interested in the conversation.

Second, you can use nonverbal cues to show that you are listening. Nodding your head and smiling at appropriate moments can signal that you follow along and understand what the speaker is saying. Mirroring the speaker's body language can also effectively convey that you are engaged in the conversation.

Third, you can use verbal cues to demonstrate that you are listening. For example, you can repeat key points to the speaker in your own words to show that you understand what they are saying. This can also help clarify any misunderstandings and ensure you are on the same page. Asking questions and providing feedback are also effective verbal cues that show you actively listen.

It's important to note that showing you are listening without interrupting requires patience and practice. Interjecting with your thoughts and opinions can be tempting, but it's important to let the speaker finish their thoughts before responding. By actively listening and showing that you are engaged in the conversation, you can improve your communication skills and build stronger relationships with those around you.

FURTHER LISTENING SKILLS

Good communication is a two-way street that involves both speaking and listening. While we have already discussed the importance of active listening and how to avoid interrupting, there is much more to becoming a skilled listener. In this chapter, we'll dive deeper into the art of listening and explore different listening skills. By understanding how to listen to emotions, interpret nonverbal cues, read between the lines, and respond effectively, we can become better communicators and build stronger relationships. So, let's get started on our journey to become master listeners.

LISTENING FOR EMOTIONS

Listening to emotions is a critical skill that can enhance our understanding of others and improve communication. Emotions are an essential part of our communication; they can convey meaning beyond our words. As a result, it's necessary to listen to the emotions behind the words to better understand what the person is trying to communicate.

To listen for emotions, we need to pay attention to the tone of voice, volume, and pace of the speaker's speech. These factors can provide clues to the emotional state of the speaker. For example, if someone speaks loudly and aggressively, they may be angry or frustrated. Alternatively, if someone is speaking softly and slowly, they may be sad or upset.

Another way to listen to emotions is to pay attention to the person's words. Some words and phrases can indicate a particular emotion, such as "I'm so excited," "I'm disappointed," or "I'm feeling anxious." By listening carefully to these words and phrases, we can gain insight into the speaker's emotional state.

It's important to note that emotions can be complex and multi-layered, so it's not always easy to identify them accurately. However, with practice and patience, we can develop our ability to listen to emotions and improve our communication skills.

By listening for emotions, we can better understand the needs and wants of the person we're speaking with. This understanding can help us respond appropriately and empathetically, leading to more positive and meaningful interactions. Additionally, by acknowledging and validating the emotions of others, we can build trust and rapport, leading to stronger and more satisfying relationships.

IDENTIFYING NONVERBAL CUES

Nonverbal cues are a crucial aspect of communication. They can provide insight into a speaker's thoughts, feelings, and intentions, even when their words say something different. Identifying nonverbal cues is an essential listening skill to help you better understand and interpret what someone is saying.

Nonverbal communication includes many behaviors, such as facial expressions, body language, gestures, tone of voice, and eye contact. Each of these behaviors can convey information about a speaker's emotional state, level of interest or engagement, and even honesty.

One of the key benefits of identifying nonverbal cues is that they can help you determine when someone is not being truthful or is hiding something. For example, if a person is saying one thing, but their body language and tone of voice indicate something different, it may be a sign that they are not being entirely honest.

Additionally, nonverbal cues can provide insight into a speaker's emotional state. For instance, if someone appears nervous, agitated, or uncomfortable during a conversation, it may indicate feeling stressed or anxious. Conversely, if someone is relaxed, smiling, and making eye contact, it may mean that they are feeling comfortable and engaged in the conversation.

To identify nonverbal cues, paying close attention to the speaker's body language, facial expressions, and tone of voice is essential. For example, if someone avoids eye contact or crosses their arms, it may be a sign that they are defensive or uncomfortable. Alternatively, if someone is leaning in, nodding, or making frequent hand gestures, it may indicate that they are engaged and interested in the conversation.

Identifying nonverbal cues is an essential listening skill to help you better understand and interpret what someone is saying. By paying attention to a speaker's body language, facial expressions, and tone of voice, you can gain valuable insights into their thoughts, feelings, and intentions, ultimately improving your communication ability.

HOW TO READ BETWEEN THE LINES

Sometimes what is not said is just as important as what is displayed. This is where the ability to read between the lines becomes a valuable listening skill. When someone is communicating, they may not always express everything they are thinking or feeling directly. There may be underlying emotions or messages that are not explicitly stated, and it is up to the listener to pick up on these cues.

Here are some tips for reading between the lines:

1.   Pay attention to nonverbal cues: Nonverbal communication can often reveal more than what is said. Facial expressions, body language, tone of voice, and gestures can explain the speaker's underlying emotions or messages. For example, a person may say they are "fine" when asked how they are doing, but their slumped shoulders and downcast gaze may indicate that they are feeling sad or down.

2.   Listen for what is not being said: Sometimes, the most important information is what is not being displayed. Pay attention to gaps in the speaker's message or topics they may avoid. For example, a friend may talk about their weekend but avoid mentioning their partner, which may indicate trouble in their relationship.

3.   Consider the context: The context in which a message is delivered can provide important clues to the underlying meaning. Consider the speaker's tone, the setting, and any other factors

influencing the message. For example, a person may express excitement about a new job but sound hesitant or unsure when discussing the details.

4.   Ask clarifying questions: If you suspect there is more to the message than what is being said, ask clarifying questions. Use open-ended questions to encourage the speaker to elaborate or provide more information. For example, you might say, "Can you tell me more about how that made you feel?"

Reading between the lines requires a combination of active listening and attention to nonverbal cues. By developing this skill, you can better understand what others are thinking and feeling and become a more effective communicator.

PARAPHRASING AND SUMMARIZING

Paraphrasing and summarizing are two crucial listening skills that can help us better understand the message and respond appropriately. Paraphrasing involves restating the speaker's message in our own words while summarizing involves condensing the message into its key points. Both skills require active listening and a deep understanding of the speaker's message.

One benefit of paraphrasing and summarizing is that they demonstrate to the speaker that we are actively listening and trying to understand their message. This can help to build trust and rapport between the speaker and the listener, as it shows that the listener is genuinely interested in what the speaker has to say.

Another benefit of these skills is that they help to clarify any misunderstandings or confusion. By restating or condensing the message, the listener can check their understanding and ensure that they have accurately grasped the speaker's intended message. This can prevent miscommunication and misunderstandings, leading to conflict and damage relationships.

To effectively paraphrase and summarize, it is important to use your own words while staying true to the speaker's message. This requires active listening and careful attention to detail. Additionally, it can be helpful to ask the speaker for clarification or feedback to ensure that you have accurately captured their message.

Overall, paraphrasing and summarizing are valuable listening skills that can help to build trust and understanding in communication. By mastering these skills, we can become more effective listeners and improve our relationships with others.

HOW TO RESPOND EFFECTIVELY TO WHAT YOU HEAR

How we respond to what we hear is just as important as how we listen. Responding effectively can help to build stronger relationships, deepen understanding, and prevent misunderstandings. This section will explore how to respond effectively to what you hear.

1.   Acknowledge and Validate The first step in responding effectively is to acknowledge what you've heard and validate the

speaker's feelings. This can be as simple as saying, "I understand how you feel," or "That sounds difficult." Validating someone's feelings lets them know that you're listening and that you understand where they're coming from.

2.   Paraphrase and Clarify Another effective way to respond to what you hear is to paraphrase and clarify. This involves restating what the speaker has said in your own words to ensure that you understand them correctly. It also shows the speaker that you are actively listening and trying to understand their perspective. For example, you might say, "So, if I understand you correctly, you feel frustrated because you haven't been given enough information about the project."

3.   Empathize Empathy is the ability to understand and share the feelings of others. Responding with empathy can help to build rapport and trust with the speaker. To show empathy, you might say, "I can imagine how difficult that must be for you," or "I would feel the same way in your situation."

4.   Offer Support Sometimes, the best response is to offer support. This might involve asking the speaker if they need help or offering encouragement. For example, you might say, "Is there anything I can do to help you?" or "I believe in you, and I know you can get through this."

5.   Avoid Judgment and Advice Finally; it's important to avoid responding with judgment or unsolicited advice. This can make the speaker feel defensive or dismissed. Instead, focus on acknowledging and validating their feelings and offering support.

Using these techniques, we can respond effectively to what we hear and build stronger relationships with those around us. It takes practice and patience to master these skills, but we can become better listeners and more effective communicators with time.

In a world that often emphasizes the importance of speaking and being heard, it's easy to overlook the power of listening. However, effective communication is a two-way street that requires both speaking and listening. By honing our listening skills and becoming more attentive, we can deepen our relationships, better understand the people around us, and communicate more effectively.

In this chapter, we've explored various techniques for further developing our listening skills. We've discussed listening for emotions, identifying nonverbal cues, reading between the lines, paraphrasing and summarizing, and responding effectively to what we hear. By implementing these strategies, we can improve our ability to truly listen and understand others, building stronger connections and enhancing our communication skills. So let's commit to becoming better listeners and reap the rewards of stronger, more meaningful relationships.

EGO SUSPENSION AND SOCIAL CONNECTION

Are you tired of feeling like you're constantly butting heads with others in your conversations? Maybe it's time to try a different approach. Ego suspension could be the key to unlocking meaningful connections with those around you. In this chapter, we'll delve into what ego suspension means, its benefits, and techniques you can use to put it into practice. By embracing ego suspension, you can improve your communication skills and create more authentic and fulfilling relationships. We'll also explore the role of empathy in ego suspension and how it can help you connect with others on a deeper level.

WHAT IS EGO SUSPENSION?

Ego suspension is the practice of setting aside one's biases, beliefs, and assumptions during a conversation to listen and understand the other person's perspective truly. It requires the ability to recognize and acknowledge that our own experiences and beliefs may not be the only ones and that other people's views are just as valid.

The concept of ego suspension is closely related to active listening, in which the listener fully engages with the speaker and strives to understand their point of view without judgment or interruption. Ego suspension takes active listening one step further by acknowledging and setting aside one's preconceptions, prejudices, and emotional reactions during the conversation.

By suspending our egos, we create a safe space for others to express their thoughts and feelings without fear of judgment or rejection. This can lead to more honest and open communication, deeper understanding, and stronger relationships.

Ego suspension is not an easy practice, as it requires much self-awareness and discipline. It may be not easy to let go of our beliefs and opinions, especially if we feel strongly about them. However, practice allows us to set our egos aside and truly listen to others with an open mind and heart.

THE BENEFITS OF EGO SUSPENSION

Ego suspension is setting aside one's needs and desires to engage and empathize with others fully. It involves putting the needs and perspectives of others first without judgment or bias. While it may seem counterintuitive to set aside one's ego, there are many benefits to practicing ego suspension.

One of the main benefits of ego suspension is that it can help to build stronger relationships with others. By showing that we are willing to listen to others and understand their perspective, we create a sense of trust and respect. This can lead to more open and honest communication and ultimately deepen our connections with others.

Another benefit of ego suspension is that it can help to reduce conflicts and misunderstandings. When we can suspend our ego and listen to others, we are more likely to identify and address potential conflicts before they escalate. This can help foster a more positive and peaceful environment at home and in the workplace.

Ego suspension can also help us to learn and grow as individuals. When we are open to hearing other perspectives, we may discover new ideas and insights we had not considered before. This can lead to personal growth and development and a greater appreciation for the diversity of thoughts and experiences in the world.

Practicing ego suspension can bring many benefits, including stronger relationships, reduced conflicts, and personal growth. By setting aside our egos and focusing on others, we can create more positive and fulfilling interactions with those around us.

TECHNIQUES FOR PRACTICING EGO SUSPENSION

Techniques for practicing ego suspension can be very helpful in improving our social connections and communication with others. Ego suspension is setting aside one's beliefs, opinions, and feelings to focus on the other person and their perspective. This can be not easy, as we are often attached to our beliefs and opinions. However, there are several techniques we can use to practice ego suspension:

1.   Mindful listening: When you are engaged in a conversation with someone, practice actively listening to what they are saying without interrupting or thinking about how you will respond. Focus solely on the speaker and try to understand their perspective.

2.   Ask open-ended questions: Rather than making assumptions or jumping to conclusions, ask open-ended questions encouraging the other person to share more about their thoughts and feelings. This can help you gain a deeper understanding of their perspective and show them that you are interested in what they say.

3.   Practice empathy: Empathy involves putting yourself in someone else's shoes and imagining how they might feel in a given situation. By practicing empathy, you can better understand where the other person is coming from and show them that you care about their feelings.

4.   Validate their feelings: If someone is sharing something personal or emotional with you, it can be helpful to validate their feelings by acknowledging them and showing empathy. This can help the other person feel heard and understood.

5.   Be open to learning: Ego suspension involves being open to new ideas and perspectives. Be willing to learn from others and challenge your assumptions and beliefs.

Practicing ego suspension requires a willingness to set aside our ego and focus on the other person. Using these techniques, we can become better listeners and improve our social connections.

HOW TO CONNECT WITH OTHERS THROUGH EGO SUSPENSION

Ego suspension is temporarily setting aside your beliefs, opinions, and attitudes to listen to and understand others. When you practice ego suspension, you consciously try to see things from the other person's perspective and hear their thoughts and feelings without judgment. Doing so creates a safe space for the other person to express themselves and connect with them on a deeper level.

To connect with others through ego suspension, it's important to start by acknowledging that you don't have all the answers and that there are multiple perspectives on any given topic. This mindset will allow you to approach conversations with an open mind and a willingness to learn from others. It's also important to practice active listening, which involves giving the other person your full attention, asking clarifying questions, and showing genuine interest in what they say.

Another key component of connecting with others through ego suspension is being aware of your biases and assumptions. We all have unconscious biases and beliefs that can influence our perceptions and judgments of others. By recognizing and acknowledging these biases, you can work to overcome them and see things from a more objective perspective.

Practicing empathy is important to connect with others through ego suspension. Empathy involves putting yourself in the other person's shoes and trying to understand their thoughts and feelings from their perspective. This involves being attentive to their nonverbal cues, such as body language, tone of voice, and words. Demonstrating empathy can create a sense of mutual understanding and build stronger relationships with others.

Connecting with others through ego suspension involves approaching conversations with an open mind, practicing active listening, being aware of your biases and assumptions, and demonstrating empathy. Doing so can create a safe space for others to express themselves and build deeper connections with those around you.

THE ROLE OF EMPATHY IN EGO SUSPENSION

Empathy is a crucial aspect of ego suspension and plays a vital role in fostering social connections. Empathy refers to the ability to understand and share another person's feelings. It involves being aware of the emotions that someone else is experiencing and connecting with them on an emotional level. In the context of ego suspension, empathy means setting aside our own beliefs, opinions, and experiences and actively listening to others to understand their perspectives and feelings.

When we practice empathy, we create a safe space for others to express themselves. It allows us to see things from their point of view and understand how their experiences shape their beliefs and values. This can be especially valuable when we're in a conflict or disagreement with someone else. We can deescalate the situation and find common ground by listening with empathy.

Empathy also helps us build stronger relationships with others. We create a deeper connection with them when we show that we care about their experiences and feelings. This connection fosters trust, which is crucial for building healthy relationships. When we practice ego suspension, we're not just showing empathy; we're actively seeking it out. We're asking others to share their experiences and perspectives with us, and we're listening with an open mind and heart.

Ultimately, the role of empathy in ego suspension is to foster social connections. By suspending our egos and practicing empathy, we create a space where others feel seen, heard, and valued. We show that we care about them as people and are willing to put our beliefs and opinions aside to connect with them on a deeper level. Doing so creates the foundation for healthy, meaningful relationships that can last a lifetime.

As you work on implementing ego suspension in your daily interactions, don't forget the crucial role of empathy in the process. By truly understanding and acknowledging the feelings and perspectives of others, you can create a space of trust and respect that allows for genuine connection. You can break down barriers through ego suspension and empathy and build meaningful relationships with those around you. So take the time to practice and develop these skills, and watch as your communication and social connections flourish.

HOW TO NEVER HAVE A BAD INTERACTION

Do you often find yourself replaying a conversation in your head, wishing you had responded differently or avoided a misunderstanding? We all experience communication mishaps and conflicts daily, but it doesn't have to be that way. In this chapter, we'll provide practical tools and strategies to help you navigate any interaction successfully. We'll discuss common communication mistakes to avoid, how to recover from a misstep, tips for avoiding misunderstandings, and strategies for de-escalating conflicts. Additionally, we'll delve into the power of forgiveness and understanding to help you move past any lingering negative interactions. With these insights, you can be confident never to have a bad interaction again.

COMMON COMMUNICATION MISTAKES TO AVOID

When it comes to communication, there are several common mistakes that people tend to make that can lead to misunderstandings, hurt feelings, and damaged relationships. By being aware of these mistakes, you can avoid them and improve the quality of your interactions with others.

1.   Not Listening: One of the most common communication mistakes is not listening actively to what the other person is saying. This can lead to misunderstandings and misinterpretations of their message.

2.   Interrupting: Interrupting the other person while speaking can be perceived as rude and disrupt the flow of the conversation.

3.   Being defensive: Being defensive when receiving feedback or criticism can hinder productive communication and make the other person feel dismissed or unheard.

4.   Assuming: Making assumptions about the other person's meaning without seeking clarification can lead to misunderstandings and miscommunications.

5.   Failing to be clear: Not being clear in your communication can lead to confusion and misunderstandings. It is important to be clear and concise in your message to ensure it is understood.

6.   Not considering the other person's perspective: Failing to consider the other person's point of view can lead to a breakdown in communication and make them feel unheard or invalidated.

7.   Using aggressive or hurtful language: Using aggressive or hostile language can be damaging to the other person and can escalate conflict rather than resolve it.

By being aware of these common communication mistakes, you can work towards avoiding them and improving the quality of your interactions with others.

HOW TO RECOVER FROM A COMMUNICATION MISSTEP

Recovering from a communication misstep is an important skill, as it can help salvage a conversation or interaction that has gone off track. People make many common communication mistakes, and it's important to be aware of them to recover from them effectively.

One common communication mistake is interrupting. Interrupting someone can be frustrating and disrespectful, derailing a conversation. If you find yourself interrupting someone, it's important to apologize and allow them to finish their thoughts.

Another common mistake is failing to listen actively. When we're not actively listening, we may miss important information or fail to understand someone's perspective. If you realize you haven't been actively listening, try to refocus your attention and ask the person to repeat what they said.

Using aggressive or confrontational language is also a common communication mistake. This can escalate a conflict and make it more difficult to resolve. If you find yourself using aggressive language, take a step back and try rephrasing your words more neutrally or diplomatically.

Talking too much and not allowing others to speak is another communication mistake that can hinder effective communication. If you find yourself dominating the conversation, try to take a step back and encourage others to share their thoughts.

Once you've identified a communication mistake, it's important to take steps to recover from it. This may involve apologizing for any disrespect or hurt feelings caused by error and actively working to understand the other person's perspective. You may need to take a break from the conversation to give everyone involved time to relax and reflect on the situation.

Overall, recovering from a communication misstep requires self-awareness, empathy, and a willingness to take responsibility for our actions. By avoiding common communication mistakes and working to recover from errors, we can build stronger relationships and avoid bad interactions in the future.

TIPS FOR AVOIDING MISUNDERSTANDINGS

Misunderstandings can occur when the sender's intended message differs from the receiver's interpretation. They can lead to confusion, frustration, and even conflict. To avoid misunderstandings, it's important to be aware of the common communication mistakes that can contribute to them. Here are some tips for avoiding misunderstandings:

1.	Use clear and concise language: One of the most common mistakes that can lead to misunderstandings is using vague or unclear language. Be specific in what you say, and avoid using jargon or technical terms that others may not understand.

2.   Check for understanding: Before assuming that the other person has understood your message, take the time to confirm that they have. Ask open-ended questions that encourage others to share their thoughts and feelings.

3.   Avoid assumptions: Assuming that the other person knows what you're discussing can lead to misunderstandings. Don't assume that the other person has the same knowledge or understanding as you do. Instead, clarify any unfamiliar terms or concepts.

4.   Pay attention to nonverbal cues: Nonverbal cues, such as facial expressions and body language, can provide valuable information about how the other person interprets your message. Be aware of these cues and adjust your message accordingly.

5.   Be mindful of your tone: Your voice can convey the meaning that may not be apparent in your words. Be aware of your tone and adjust it to ensure that your message is being received as intended.

6.   Use examples: Providing examples can help clarify your message and make it more relatable. Use models that are relevant to the other person's experiences or interests.

By avoiding these common communication mistakes and using these tips for avoiding misunderstandings, you can improve the clarity and effectiveness of your communication and prevent unnecessary conflicts.

STRATEGIES FOR DE-ESCALATING CONFLICT

Conflicts are a natural part of human interaction, and knowing how to manage them effectively is important. Conflict can arise from a difference of opinion, a miscommunication, or even a misunderstanding of intentions. Whatever the cause, how you handle conflict can significantly impact the outcome of the interaction.

Here are some common communication mistakes that can escalate conflicts:

1.   Being defensive: When you feel attacked, it's natural to want to defend yourself. However, defensiveness can lead to a breakdown in communication and make the conflict worse.

2.   Interrupting: Interrupting the other person can be seen as disrespectful and dismissive, and it can escalate the conflict.

3.   Blaming: Blaming the other person for the conflict can make them defensive and escalate the conflict.

4.   Not listening: Not listening to the other person can make them feel unheard and escalate the conflict.

5.   Name-calling: Name-calling can be hurtful and disrespectful, escalating the conflict.

To de-escalate conflicts, here are some strategies you can use:

1.   Stay calm: When you're relaxed, you can think clearly and respond rationally.

2.   Listen actively: Active listening involves paying attention to the other person, acknowledging their feelings, and repeating what they've said to show that you understand.

3.   Use "I" statements: Using "I" statements can help you express your feelings without blaming the other person. For example, instead of saying, "You never listen to me," say, "I feel like you're not listening to me."

4.   Find common ground: Look for areas of agreement and build on them. This can help you find a solution that works for both parties.

5.   Take a break: If the conflict is escalating and you're not progressing, it may be time to take a break and return to the conversation later.

By avoiding common communication mistakes and using de-escalation strategies, you can learn how to manage conflicts effectively and avoid bad interactions. Remember, conflicts are a natural part of human interaction, but with the right tools and strategies, you can learn how to handle them to foster understanding and strengthen relationships.

THE POWER OF FORGIVENESS AND UNDERSTANDING

The power of forgiveness and understanding is a crucial aspect of effective communication, especially when avoiding harmful interactions. Forgiveness allows individuals to overcome a conflict or misunderstanding and build stronger relationships.

Understanding will enable individuals to empathize with others and create mutual account.

However, before discussing the power of forgiveness and understanding, it's important first to identify some common communication mistakes that can lead to bad interactions. Here are some of the most common communication mistakes to avoid:

1.   Jumping to conclusions: When we assume we know what someone will say or mean, we are more likely to misunderstand them.

2.   Failing to listen: Not listening to the other person can lead to misunderstandings, hurt feelings, and a communication breakdown.

3.   Blaming or attacking: When we blame or attack the other person, it puts them on the defensive and can escalate the conflict.

4.   Making assumptions: Assuming we know what the other person is thinking or feeling can lead to misunderstandings and missed opportunities for connection.

5.   Not taking responsibility: Refusing responsibility for our actions or words can prevent us from resolving conflicts and moving forward.

Now, let's explore the power of forgiveness and understanding in communication. Forgiveness involves letting go of resentment or anger towards someone who has wronged us. When we forgive someone, we are not excusing their behavior, but rather, we are freeing ourselves from the negative emotions associated with the situation. Forgiveness can improve mental health, reduce stress, and strengthen relationships.

On the other hand, understanding involves empathizing with others and trying to see things from their perspective. Understanding someone makes us more likely to be patient, compassionate, and forgiving. Understanding can lead to greater connection, better communication, and improved relationships.

To harness the power of forgiveness and understanding in our communication, it's important to practice active listening, empathy, and compassion. We should also strive to be open-minded and willing to see things from the other person's perspective. When conflicts arise, we should try to focus on finding a solution rather than placing blame or attacking the other person.

Overall, forgiveness and understanding are essential for avoiding bad interactions and building stronger relationships. By avoiding common communication mistakes, practicing empathy and active listening, and focusing on finding solutions rather than placing blame, we can harness this power and create more positive interactions in our daily lives.

In conclusion, by being aware of common communication mistakes, learning to recover from missteps, avoiding misunderstandings, de-escalating conflict, and practicing forgiveness and understanding, you can learn how never to have a bad interaction again. These tools and strategies can improve your communication skills and help you build stronger relationships with others.

MASTERING THE ART OF SMALL TALK

Picture this: You're at a party, standing alone in the corner, feeling like you're the only one without anyone to talk to. You glance around the room, hoping someone will approach you, but everyone seems deep in conversation with someone else. Sound familiar? The truth is that small talk is a vital part of building relationships and making connections, whether in your personal or professional life. In this chapter, we'll unlock the secrets to mastering the art of small talk, including techniques for starting a conversation, how to keep it going, strategies for finding common ground, and tips for gracefully ending a conversation. So, if you want to become a skilled conversationalist and never feel awkward at a social event again, read on!

WHY SMALL TALK IS IMPORTANT?

Small talk often gets a bad reputation as meaningless and shallow conversation. However, it serves an important purpose in our social interactions. Small talk can be a way to establish a connection with someone, demonstrate interest, and even build trust. It can serve as an icebreaker, a way to ease into a conversation, and a way to gauge someone's interests and personality.

Small talk can also play a significant role in networking and professional settings. When meeting new people in a professional environment, starting with small talk can be a way to build rapport and establish common ground. It can demonstrate your social skills, confidence, and ability to connect with others, which can be valuable in building professional relationships and advancing your career.

Moreover, small talk can be a great way to practice active listening and communication skills. When engaged in small talk, you can practice asking questions, listening attentively, and responding appropriately. These skills can be valuable in both personal and professional contexts.

In short, small talk may seem insignificant, but it plays a crucial role in establishing and maintaining social connections. It can be an effective tool for building rapport, establishing common ground, and practicing communication skills.

TECHNIQUES FOR STARTING A CONVERSATION

Starting a conversation with someone new can be intimidating, but it's an important skill to master for building relationships and networking. Here are some techniques to help you start a conversation:

1.   Make an observation: Look around your environment and find something interesting to comment on. It could be the decor, the weather, or something the person is wearing or holding.

2.   Ask a question: Ask an open-ended question to get the conversation flowing. This could be something related to the event or context or about the person's interests or experiences.

3.   Compliment: Give a genuine praise to the person you're talking to. This could be about their outfit, their work, or something they've achieved.

4.   Introduce yourself: If you don't know the person you want to talk to, introduce yourself and ask for their name. This can be a good way to break the ice and start a conversation.

5.   Use a conversation starter: There are many conversation starters available online that you can use to start a conversation. Some examples include "What's your favorite movie?" or "If you could go anywhere in the world, where would you go?"

Remember, being genuine and curious is the key to starting a conversation. People can usually tell when someone is going through the motions, so make sure you are genuinely interested in what the person says. Using these techniques, you can start a conversation with anyone and make a connection that could lead to a lasting relationship.

HOW TO KEEP A CONVERSATION GOING

Small talk can be intimidating for many people, but one of the biggest challenges is keeping the conversation flowing. Once you've initiated a conversation, keeping the other person engaged and interested is important. Here are some tips for keeping a conversation going:

1.   Listen actively: One of the most important aspects of keeping a conversation going is listening to what the other person is saying. Pay attention to their words, tone of voice, and body

language. This will help you keep the conversation going and make the other person feel heard and valued.

2.   Ask open-ended questions: Asking open-ended questions encourages the other person to share more information and can lead to more interesting conversations. Avoid asking yes or no questions, as they can quickly bring the conversation to a halt. Instead, ask questions requiring more in-depth answers and encourage others to share their thoughts and experiences.

3.   Share your experiences: Sharing your experiences or opinions can also keep the conversation going. However, be mindful of dominating the conversation or making it all about you. Make sure to also ask the other person about their experiences and opinions.

4.   Find common ground: Look for common interests or experiences you can bond over. This can help you both feel more comfortable and connected and provide more topics for conversation.

5.   Be curious: Show genuine curiosity about the other person and their life. Ask questions about their job, hobbies, or family. This can help build rapport and create a more enjoyable conversation for both of you.

6.   Stay positive: Keep the conversation positive and avoid complaining or being overly negative. This can quickly turn the other person off and end the conversation prematurely.

7.   Use humor: Humor can be a great way to keep conversation light and engaging. However, be careful not to offend or upset the other person with inappropriate or insensitive jokes.

With these tips in mind, you can master the art of keeping a conversation going and become a skilled conversationalist in any situation.

STRATEGIES FOR FINDING COMMON GROUND IN SMALL TALK

Small talk is often perceived as superficial, but it can be an excellent way to connect with others, find common ground, and build relationships. One of the keys to successful small talk is finding common ground with the person you're talking to. Having shared interests or experiences makes it much easier to have a meaningful conversation.

Here are some strategies for finding common ground in small talk:

1.   Look for clues: Observe your surroundings and the person you're talking to for clues about their interests, hobbies, or profession. For example, if you're at a networking event, you might notice someone wearing a pin or shirt related to a particular industry or cause. Use these clues as an opening to start a conversation and find out more about their interests.

2.   Ask open-ended questions: Ask questions that require more than a yes or no answer. For example, instead of asking, "Do

you like sports?" you could ask, "What's your favorite sport to watch or play?" This encourages the other person to share more about themselves, and you may discover a shared interest.

3.   Share your own experiences: When you share your own experiences or interests, it can prompt the other person to share theirs. For example, if you're talking about a recent vacation, you could mention a particular activity or sightseeing spot you enjoyed and ask if they've ever been to that destination or done that activity.

4.   Listen actively: Pay attention to what the other person is saying, and show genuine interest in their responses. This can help you find common ground and keep the conversation flowing.

5.   Look for similarities, not differences: It's easy to focus on and dwell on differences, but finding common ground requires focusing on similarities. Look for shared experiences, interests, or perspectives, and use these as a starting point for conversation.

Using these strategies, you can find common ground with almost anyone and make small talk less awkward and more meaningful. Remember, small talk is just the beginning of building a relationship, but it's an important first step.

TIPS FOR ENDING A CONVERSATION GRACEFULLY

Small talk can be a great way to establish a connection with someone, but eventually, you will need to end the conversation. It's important to know how to do this gracefully so you don't leave a bad impression or come across as rude. Here are some tips for ending a conversation on a positive note:

1.   Use a natural transition: Look for a natural break in the conversation, such as when the other person finishes a thought or pauses to breathe. This is a good opportunity to smoothly end the conversation by saying, "Well, it was great talking with you, but I need to go check on something."

2.   Offer a compliment or thank them: A praise or expression of gratitude can be a nice way to end a conversation. You could say something like, "Thanks for sharing your thoughts on that; I appreciated it," or "It was great meeting you; I hope we can chat again soon."

3.   Make plans: If you enjoyed talking to the person and want to continue the conversation or get to know them better, suggest making plans. This could be as simple as exchanging contact information or setting a specific time and place to meet again.

4.   Be polite: Regardless of the reason for ending the conversation, being polite and respectful is important. Thank the person for their time and letting them know you enjoyed talking with them. Avoid abruptly ending the conversation or walking away without saying goodbye.

5.   Pay attention to body language: If the other person seems ready to end the conversation, pay attention to their body language. If they look around or seem distracted, it may be time to wrap things up. Similarly, if they seem engaged and interested

in continuing the conversation, you can keep talking for a bit longer.

By following these tips, you can gracefully end a small talk conversation and leave a positive impression on the other person. Remember, small talk is an important skill to develop for building relationships and networking, but it's also important to know when it's time to move on to other things.

In conclusion, mastering the art of small talk can be a valuable skill for building relationships, networking, and establishing connections with others. Using the techniques, strategies, and tips outlined in this chapter, you can become a skilled conversationalist and feel more comfortable and confident in social and professional situations.

AVOIDING THE MISTAKES

Are you tired of miscommunications and damaged relationships? Do you want to improve your communication skills and avoid common mistakes that can lead to misunderstandings? Look no further than this chapter! In the following pages, we'll delve into people's most common communication mistakes, providing tips and techniques for avoiding them. We'll also discuss how to repair damaged relationships, offer advice on giving and receiving feedback, and explore empathy's powerful role in avoiding mistakes altogether. Let's get started!

COMMON COMMUNICATION MISTAKES TO AVOID

Effective communication is a critical aspect of our daily lives, and avoiding common communication mistakes can greatly improve our relationships and interactions with others. Communication mistakes can range from minor word choice or tone errors to more significant misunderstandings that can damage relationships. In this subchapter, we will discuss some common communication mistakes to avoid.

1.   Not listening actively: Active listening is an essential component of effective communication. Failing to listen actively can lead to misunderstandings and make others feel ignored or unimportant. It is important to give your full attention to the person speaking and avoid distractions.

2.   Making assumptions: Making assumptions can lead to misunderstandings and can damage relationships. Assuming that

you understand what the other person is saying or thinking without asking for clarification can lead to miscommunication and frustration.

3.   Using negative language: Negative language can have a detrimental effect on communication. Using accusatory, judgmental, or critical language can create defensiveness and cause the other person to shut down.

4.   Interrupting: Interrupting someone while speaking can be disrespectful and lead to misunderstandings. Interrupting can also make the other person feel like their thoughts or feelings are not valued.

5.   Not expressing yourself clearly: Failing to express yourself clearly can lead to misunderstandings and confusion. It is important to use clear and concise language and to avoid vague or ambiguous statements.

6.   Not being aware of nonverbal communication: Nonverbal communication, such as body language and tone of voice, can significantly impact communication. Failing to be mindful of nonverbal cues can lead to misunderstandings and can make the other person feel like their message is not being heard or understood.

7.   Not asking questions: Failing to ask questions can lead to misunderstandings and make the other person feel like their thoughts or feelings are not valued. Asking questions can help

clarify misunderstandings and demonstrate a willingness to understand the other person's perspective.

In conclusion, avoiding common communication mistakes can greatly improve our relationships and interactions. It is essential to be aware of these mistakes and to take steps to prevent them. By actively listening, avoiding assumptions, using positive language, not interrupting, expressing yourself clearly, being aware of nonverbal communication, and asking questions, you can become a more effective communicator and build stronger relationships with those around you.

HOW TO AVOID MISUNDERSTANDINGS

Misunderstandings can cause much frustration and can damage relationships. They often occur when we assume the other person knows what we mean or don't take the time to clarify our message. However, there are several techniques that we can use to avoid misunderstandings.

1.   Be clear and concise: When communicating, it's important to be clear and concise. Don't use complex language or jargon the other person may not understand. Instead, use simple, easy-to-understand language that gets your message across clearly.

2.   Repeat and confirm: It's always a good idea to repeat and demonstrate what the other person is saying to ensure you've understood them correctly. This shows that you actively listen and care about what they say.

3.   Ask questions: If you're unsure what the other person means, ask questions to clarify. Don't make assumptions or jump to conclusions without checking your understanding.

4.   Use examples: If you're trying to explain something difficult to understand, using examples can be helpful. This can make the information more relatable and easier to comprehend.

5.   Check for cultural differences: Different cultures have different communication styles and norms. If you're communicating with someone from a different culture, take the time to understand their communication style and adjust your approach accordingly.

6.   Avoid distractions: It's important to avoid distractions when communicating. Turn off your phone or put it on silent, avoid multitasking, and give the other person your full attention.

By following these techniques, we can minimize misunderstandings and ensure effective communication. It's important to remember that effective communication requires effort and attention, but it's worth it, in the long run, to build stronger relationships and avoid unnecessary conflicts.

TIPS FOR GIVING AND RECEIVING FEEDBACK

Giving and receiving feedback is a crucial part of effective communication. Feedback helps individuals improve their performance, understand their strengths and weaknesses, and adjust as needed. However, giving and receiving feedback can be difficult, especially if the input is negative or critical. This subchapter will explore some tips for effectively giving and receiving feedback.

Tips for Giving Feedback

1.   Be specific: When giving feedback, it's important to be clear about what the person did well or needs to improve. General feedback such as "good job" or "you need to improve" is not helpful. Be specific about what was good or what needs improvement. For example, instead of saying, "Good job on the project," say, "I appreciated how you took the initiative to research and include additional data in the project. It helped to strengthen our findings."

2.   Be timely: Feedback should be given promptly. Waiting too long can reduce the effectiveness of the feedback and make it seem less relevant. For example, if you notice a colleague struggling with a particular task, it's best to provide feedback as soon as possible so they can make the necessary adjustments.

3.   Be constructive: Feedback should be productive and aimed at helping the person improve. Avoid being overly critical or harsh. Focus on providing helpful and actionable feedback that will assist the person in achieving their goals.

4.   Be empathetic: Feedback can be difficult to hear, especially negative. Try to put yourself in the person's shoes and provide feedback in an empathetic and supportive way. Use language that shows you understand their perspective and acknowledge their efforts.

Tips for Receiving Feedback

1. Be open-minded: When receiving feedback, it's important to approach it open-mindedly. Be willing to listen to the feedback and consider its value. Avoid becoming defensive or dismissive of the input.

2. Ask clarifying questions: If you're unsure about the feedback, ask for clarification. Ask questions to help you understand the feedback and what you can do to improve.

3. Accepting feedback can be difficult, but it's important to take ownership of your actions and behaviors. Don't make excuses or shift blame. Instead, acknowledge the feedback and take responsibility for making improvements.

4. Follow up: After receiving feedback, following up with the person who provided it is important. Let them know how you plan to use their feedback and the progress you're making. This shows that you value their input and are committed to making changes.

Giving and receiving feedback is essential for personal and professional growth. By following these tips, you can provide and receive feedback effectively, avoid misunderstandings, and improve your communication skills. Remember, feedback should always be given and received with empathy and focused on constructive improvement.

TECHNIQUES FOR REPAIRING DAMAGED RELATIONSHIPS

Effective communication is key to building and maintaining relationships, but misunderstandings and conflicts can arise even with the best intentions. When communication has gone awry, repairing the damage and rebuilding trust can be challenging. However, with the right techniques, mending even the most damaged relationships is possible.

The first step in repairing a damaged relationship is acknowledging the problem. This means being honest with yourself and the other person about what went wrong and taking responsibility for your part. Avoid placing blame or making excuses, and instead, focus on what you can do to make things right.

Next, it's essential to listen to the other person's perspective. This means actively listening to what they say without interrupting or becoming defensive. Try to understand their point of view, and ask questions if you need clarification. Empathy is crucial in this stage, as it helps to create a safe and understanding space for the other person to express their thoughts and feelings.

After you have listened to and acknowledged the problem, it's time to work together to find a solution. This means brainstorming ideas and developing a plan that works for both parties. Avoid being too focused on your needs or desires, and be open to compromise.

Once a solution has been agreed upon, following through with the plan is important. Actions speak louder than words, and demonstrating that you are committed to making things right can help to rebuild trust and strengthen the relationship.

In addition to these techniques, it's essential to be patient and kind throughout the process. Repairing a damaged relationship takes time and effort, and giving the other person the space they need to process their emotions and come to a resolution is crucial. Remember to be respectful and understanding, even if you don't agree with their perspective.

Repairing a damaged relationship requires honesty, empathy, and commitment. Acknowledging the problem, listening to the other person's perspective, finding a solution together, and following through with the plan makes it possible to mend even the most damaged relationships. Remember that effective communication is the key to building and maintaining relationships; even the best communicators make mistakes. It is important to learn from those mistakes and use them as opportunities for growth and connection.

THE POWER OF EMPATHY IN AVOIDING MISTAKES

Empathy is a critical skill in effective communication, and it is particularly important when avoiding mistakes. Empathy involves the ability to understand and share another person's feelings, putting oneself in their shoes to gain insight into their perspective. In communication, empathy is the ability to listen actively and understand the other person's point of view, even if it differs from our own.

Empathy is crucial for avoiding mistakes because it allows us to understand how others might receive our words or actions. By putting ourselves in their shoes, we can anticipate their reactions and adjust our communication accordingly. For example, if we know that someone is going through a difficult time, we can be more mindful of our words and tone when communicating with them, avoiding anything perceived as insensitive or hurtful.

Empathy also allows us to read nonverbal cues, which can help us avoid mistakes. Often, how a person responds to our communication is more telling than the words they use. By paying attention to their body language, facial expressions, and tone of voice, we can pick up on cues indicating whether they are receptive to what we're saying or need to adjust our approach.

Another way empathy can help us avoid mistakes is by enabling us to see the bigger picture. When focused on our agenda or point of view, it can be easy to miss important details or considerations that could impact our communication. Empathy helps us broaden our perspective, considering the other person's needs, wants, limitations, and any external factors that may be influencing the situation.

Finally, empathy is essential for repairing damaged relationships. When we make mistakes in communication, it can damage our relationships with others, leading to misunderstandings, hurt feelings, and even conflict. However, when we approach the situation with empathy, we can take steps to repair the damage, demonstrating our understanding and concern for the other person's feelings. This can involve acknowledging our mistakes, apologizing sincerely, and making things right.

In summary, empathy is a powerful tool for avoiding mistakes in communication. It allows us to understand the other person's perspective, read nonverbal cues, see the bigger picture, and repair damaged relationships. By cultivating empathy in our communication, we can become more effective communicators, build stronger relationships, and avoid many common mistakes that can arise in touch.

In conclusion, avoiding common communication mistakes is essential for building and maintaining healthy relationships. You can become a more effective communicator and avoid common mistakes by identifying the most common mistakes, practicing active listening, giving and receiving feedback constructively, repairing damaged relationships, and practicing empathy. Remember, effective communication is a continual process of learning and growing, so be patient with yourself and others as you work to improve your communication skills.

AND WHEN COMMUNICATION IS DIGITAL?

In today's fast-paced digital world, most of our communication happens through digital channels such as email, social media, and text messages. While digital communication has revolutionized the way we communicate and made it easier to connect with people across the globe, it also poses a unique set of challenges. Misunderstandings, tone misinterpretation, and lack of nonverbal cues can all contribute to ineffective communication and misunderstandings. Therefore, it's crucial to understand the best practices and strategies for effective digital communication.

In this chapter, we'll explore the benefits and drawbacks of digital communication and how to navigate them to enhance your communication skills. We'll provide tips and techniques for effective email communication, strategies for making the most out of video conferencing, and communicating clearly and succinctly in a text message. Additionally, we'll delve into empathy in digital communication and how understanding and acknowledging the perspectives and emotions of the people you are communicating with can help foster better relationships and prevent misunderstandings.

THE BENEFITS AND DRAWBACKS OF DIGITAL COMMUNICATION

Digital communication has become integral to our lives, from sending emails to messaging friends on social media. However, while it has brought us closer together in many ways, it has its benefits and drawbacks.

Benefits of Digital Communication

1.   Speed: One of the biggest benefits of digital communication is speed. Messages can be sent and received almost instantaneously, allowing real-time communication regardless of distance.

2.   Convenience: Digital communication provides comfort, as people can communicate anywhere with an internet connection. This makes staying in touch with family and friends or working remotely easier.

3.   Accessible: Digital communication is accessible to almost anyone with a device and an internet connection. This allows for communication regardless of physical limitations or location.

4.   Documentation: Digital communication provides documentation of the conversation. This can be useful in business communication, where contracts and agreements must be saved and accessed later.

Drawbacks of Digital Communication

1.   Lack of nonverbal cues: One of the biggest drawbacks of digital communication is the lack of nonverbal cues. It can be difficult to convey tone or emotion through text, leading to misunderstandings or misinterpretations.

2.   Miscommunication: The lack of nonverbal cues and the potential for misunderstandings can lead to miscommunication. This can result in damaged relationships, missed opportunities, and other negative consequences.

3.   Overreliance: People can become over-reliant on digital communication, decreasing face-to-face interaction and social skills.

4.   Cybersecurity: Digital communication can also pose a risk to cybersecurity, as messages can be intercepted or hacked, compromising personal or sensitive information.

In conclusion, while digital communication has many benefits, it also has drawbacks. It is important to be aware of these drawbacks and use digital communication appropriately while valuing face-to-face communication and social skills.

BEST PRACTICES FOR EMAIL COMMUNICATION

Email communication has become an essential tool in today's digital age, and it is critical to use best practices to ensure effective communication. Here are some best practices for email communication that you should keep in mind:

1.   Use a clear and concise subject line: A clear and concise subject line helps the recipient quickly understand the purpose of the email.

2.   Keep the email short and to the point: People receive many emails daily and often don't have time to read lengthy emails. Keep your email brief and focused on the main point.

3.   Use a professional tone: It's important to maintain a professional manner in your email communication, regardless of whom you are communicating with.

4.   Use proper grammar and punctuation: Proper grammar and punctuation make your email easy to read and professional.

5.   Avoid using slang and informal language: Slang and informal language are inappropriate for professional communication and may be misunderstood.

6.   Proofread your email before sending: Always proofread your email for errors before sending it. A poorly written email can harm your reputation and credibility.

7.   Include a clear call to action: If you need the recipient to take action or reply to your email, make sure to include a clear call to action.

8.   Use the appropriate formality level: The formality level used in an email can vary depending on whom you are communicating with. Use a more formal tone for business communication and a more casual style for personal touch.

9.   Use a professional email signature: Your signature should include your name, job title, and contact information.

By following these best practices, you can improve your email communication skills and ensure that your emails are professional, clear, and effective.

STRATEGIES FOR EFFECTIVE VIDEO CONFERENCING

With the rise of remote work, video conferencing has become an increasingly important mode of communication in many workplaces. While it can be convenient and efficient, certain strategies can make video conferencing more effective.

The first strategy is ensuring you have the proper equipment and software. This includes a high-quality webcam, microphone, and speakers or headphones. Test your equipment ahead of time to make sure that you can be heard and seen clearly. Also, make sure that you have a stable internet connection.

Next, choosing an appropriate location for your video call is important. Find a quiet, well-lit space where you won't be interrupted by noise or distractions. Make sure your background is professional and not distracting. Positioning your camera at eye level is also a good idea to create a more natural and engaging conversation.

Before the call, prepare any necessary materials, such as a presentation or agenda, and share them with participants ahead of time. This will help ensure everyone is on the same page and that the call stays focused.

During the call, it's important to be engaged and present. Avoid multitasking or checking emails during the call. Instead, actively listen to others and participate in the conversation. Visual cues, such as nodding or making eye contact, can also help show that you are engaged and interested in the conversation.

Another important strategy for effective video conferencing is to practice good communication skills. This includes speaking clearly and concisely, avoiding interruptions, and being mindful of others' perspectives. Using appropriate body language and facial expressions to convey your message is also important.

Finally, after the call, it's a good idea to follow up with any necessary action items or next steps. This will help ensure that the call is productive and everyone is on the same page moving forward.

In summary, effective video conferencing requires proper equipment and preparation, an appropriate location, active engagement during the call, good communication skills, and follow-up after the call. Following these strategies can make your video calls more productive and successful.

HOW TO COMMUNICATE CLEARLY IN A TEXT MESSAGE

In today's world, text messaging has become one of the primary ways people communicate. Whether sending a quick message to a friend or colleague or engaging in a more in-depth conversation, it's important to know how to communicate effectively and clearly in a text message.

Here are some tips for communicating clearly in a text message:

1.   Keep it short and sweet: Text messages are meant to be brief, so keep them short and to the point. Avoid writing lengthy paragraphs or going off on tangents.

2.   Use proper grammar and punctuation: While text messaging may feel informal, it's still important to use appropriate grammar and punctuation. This can help prevent misunderstandings and ensure that your message is clear.

3.   Be mindful of tone: Without the benefit of nonverbal cues and tone of voice, it's easy for text messages to be misinterpreted. Be mindful of your style and use emojis or other symbols to convey your emotions if necessary.

4.   Use clear language: Avoid slang, abbreviations, or jargon the recipient may not understand. Instead, use clear and concise language that is easy to understand.

5.   Double-check before sending: Before you hit send, take a moment to read over your message and make sure it's clear and error-free. This can help prevent misunderstandings and ensure that your message is received as intended.

6.   Be responsive: Text messaging is a fast-paced form of communication, so it's important to be responsive and timely

in your replies. If you need more time to respond, let the other person know.

Following these tips, you can communicate effectively and clearly in a text message and avoid misunderstandings or misinterpretations. Remember, clear communication is key to building and maintaining strong relationships, whether they are personal or professional.

THE ROLE OF EMPATHY IN DIGITAL COMMUNICATION

As digital communication becomes increasingly prevalent in our personal and professional lives, it's important to understand empathy's role in making these interactions successful.

Empathy is the ability to understand and share the feelings of others. Empathy can be more challenging in digital communication because we often rely solely on text or instant messaging, which can easily be misinterpreted. However, by putting ourselves in the shoes of the person we're communicating with and considering their perspective, we can better understand their emotions and respond appropriately.

One way to show empathy in digital communication is to use active listening skills. This involves paying attention to the person's words and tone and responding with clarifying questions or statements that show you understand their point of view. It's also important to avoid making assumptions or jumping to conclusions, as this can lead to misunderstandings.

Another way to demonstrate empathy in digital communication is to validate the other person's feelings. For example, if someone expresses frustration or disappointment in an email, acknowledging their emotions and expressing empathy can help defuse the situation. This can be as simple as saying, "I understand why you feel that way," or "I'm sorry you're going through this."

It's also important to be mindful of our tone and language in digital communication. Sarcasm or jokes that might be well-received in person can come across as rude or offensive in text messages or emails. By choosing our words carefully and considering how they might be interpreted, we can avoid inadvertently causing harm or misunderstandings.

Finally, it's important to recognize that digital communication can never fully replace face-to-face interaction. While it's a convenient and necessary tool in many situations, it's important to make an effort to connect in person whenever possible. This can help build stronger relationships and ensure empathy is not lost in translation.

Empathy is just as important in digital communication as it is in face-to-face interactions. By actively listening, validating feelings, choosing our words carefully, and trying to connect in person, we can ensure that our digital communication is effective, respectful, and empathetic.

Digital communication has become an integral part of our lives, and it's important to use it effectively to communicate with others. By following best practices for email communication, having effective video conferences, communicating clearly in text messages, and using empathy in digital communication, we can overcome the challenges of communicating online and building strong relationships.

INTRICATE WAYS TO BE MORE CHARISMATIC

Imagine commanding attention, influencing others, and leaving a lasting impression with ease. That's the power of charisma. But what makes someone charismatic, and how can you develop this magnetic charm? In this chapter, we'll delve into the intricacies of being more charismatic, including understanding the definition of charisma, techniques for enhancing it, the power of storytelling, how to use humor to connect with others, and the critical role of confidence in boosting your charisma. So whether you're looking to ace a job interview, improve your social skills, or become more captivating in your everyday interactions, read on to discover the secrets of being a truly charismatic individual.

WHAT IS CHARISMA?

Charisma is a fascinating and elusive trait that some people possess naturally while others struggle to cultivate it. Essentially, charisma is the ability to draw others in, inspire and influence them, build rapport, and connect with them on a deep level. But what is it that makes someone charismatic?

At its core, charisma combines several key traits and behaviors that work together to create a compelling presence. These may include:

1.   Confidence: Charismatic people tend to exude confidence and self-assurance, which inspires confidence in others.

2.   Charisma is a combination of warmth and strength: Charismatic individuals are warm and approachable and project strength and authority.

3.   Good listening skills: Charismatic individuals are often great listeners, making others feel heard and valued.

4.   Being authentic: Charismatic individuals are authentic and genuine in their interactions. They don't put on air or try to be something they're not.

5.   A sense of purpose: Charismatic individuals tend to have a strong sense of purpose or mission, which can inspire others.

6.   A positive attitude: Charismatic individuals tend to be optimistic, which can be infectious and inspiring to others.

7.   Good communication skills: Charismatic individuals are often excellent communicators, able to convey their ideas and thoughts clearly and effectively.

It's important to note that charisma cannot be faked or forced. While it is possible to work on developing the key traits and behaviors associated with charisma, ultimately, it comes from within. Authenticity and genuineness are essential components of charisma; if these are lacking, it will not be easy to cultivate a truly magnetic presence.

Charisma is also context-dependent, meaning that what may be considered charismatic in one situation may not necessarily work in another. For example, the traits and behaviors associated with charisma in a business setting may differ from those that are effective in a social environment.

While there is no one-size-fits-all definition of charisma, it can be thought of as a combination of several key traits and behaviors that work together to create a compelling presence. By working on developing these traits and behaviors, individuals can become more charismatic and build stronger connections with those around them.

TECHNIQUES FOR ENHANCING CHARISMA

Charisma is a quality that can be hard to define, but we all know it when we see it. Certain people have that special quality that draws us in and makes us want to be around them. Luckily, charisma is not just something you're born with - it's a skill that can be developed and improved over time. In this section, we'll explore some techniques for enhancing your charisma.

1.   Improve your body language. Nonverbal communication is a big part of charisma. Your body language can communicate much about your confidence, interest, and engagement in a conversation. To enhance your charisma, focus on making eye contact, smiling, and using open body language. Stand up straight, with your shoulders back and your chest open.

2.   Listen actively. People with charisma are often excellent listeners. They give their full attention to the person they're speaking with, asking questions and showing genuine interest in what the other person says. To enhance your charisma, practice

active listening. Make a conscious effort to listen to what others are saying and respond thoughtfully.

3. Show vulnerability. Charismatic people are often seen as approachable and relatable. One way to enhance your charisma is to show vulnerability in your interactions with others. This doesn't mean you have to reveal your deepest secrets but be willing to share some personal stories or experiences. This can help others feel more comfortable around you and build a deeper connection.

4. Develop your sense of humor. Humor is a powerful tool for building rapport and enhancing charisma. People with charisma often have a good sense of humor and know how to use it to connect with others. To develop your sense of humor, watch and learn from funny people, practice telling jokes, and look for opportunities to inject humor into conversations.

5. Practice confidence Charismatic people are often confident in themselves and their abilities. To enhance your charisma, work on building your confidence. Set achievable goals and work towards them, celebrate your successes, and don't be afraid to take risks. When you believe in yourself, others are more likely to believe in you too.

In conclusion, enhancing your charisma is about building your communication skills, developing your confidence, and showing genuine interest and care in others. By practicing these techniques, you can improve your charisma and make deeper, more meaningful connections with the people around you.

THE POWER OF STORYTELLING IN CHARISMA

Storytelling has been an integral part of human communication for centuries. The ability to captivate an audience with a well-crafted story is a key component of charisma. Charismatic people can use stories to inspire, motivate, and connect with their audience.

Storytelling is an art form that requires practice and skill. There are a few key elements to consider when crafting a story to enhance your charisma. First, the story should be relevant to the audience. It should be relatable and resonate with the listener. This requires a keen understanding of your audience and their interests, values, and experiences.

Secondly, the story should have a clear message or moral. It should be more than just an entertaining tale; it should have a deeper meaning that the audience can take away and apply to their lives. This helps to create a connection between the storyteller and the audience.

Thirdly, the story should be engaging and well-told. Charismatic person can use their tone of voice, body language, and facial expressions to bring the story to life and make it more memorable. They should also be able to adapt their storytelling style to fit the mood and tone of the conversation.

Finally, a charismatic person should be able to use stories to illustrate their own experiences and values. Sharing personal stories can create a sense of authenticity and vulnerability that can be very attractive to others. This helps to create a deeper connection with the listener and enhances their charisma.

In summary, the power of storytelling in charisma lies in its ability to connect with an audience on a deeper level. A charismatic person can inspire and motivate others by crafting a well-told story that is relevant, has a clear message, and is engaging. Using personal stories to illustrate their experiences and values, they can create an authentic and vulnerable connection that enhances their charisma.

HOW TO USE HUMOR TO CONNECT WITH OTHERS

Humor is a powerful tool that can be used to connect with others and enhance one's charisma. A person who can make others laugh and feel at ease is often perceived as likable and approachable. However, using humor appropriately and avoiding offensive or insensitive jokes is important.

One technique for using humor to connect with others is to share personal stories that are relatable and lighthearted. These stories can help to break down barriers and make others feel more comfortable around you. It is important to remember that the goal is not to be the funniest person in the room but to use humor to build connections and establish rapport.

Another technique for using humor is to be playful and spontaneous. This can involve making witty comments or puns or finding humor in everyday situations. However, it is important to be mindful of the context and avoid making jokes that could be perceived as inappropriate or offensive.

Self-deprecating humor can also be an effective way to connect with others. Making light of one's flaws or mistakes can help break down barriers and make others feel more at ease. However, it is important to balance self-deprecating humor and self-respect and avoid being too self-critical.

In addition to these techniques, it is important to be mindful of the audience and adjust one's humor accordingly. What may be funny to one person may not be funny to another, so it is important to be sensitive to cultural and individual differences. Finally, it is important to remember that humor is just one tool in the toolbox of charisma and should be used in conjunction with other techniques, such as storytelling and confidence, to maximize its effectiveness.

THE ROLE OF CONFIDENCE IN CHARISMA

Confidence is a crucial element of charisma. When we are confident, we exude an air of self-assurance and self-belief, making us more attractive and engaging to others. A person who lacks confidence may struggle to connect with others, as they may come across as insecure or unsure of themselves.

One of the keys to developing confidence is to recognize and appreciate our strengths and abilities. This can involve taking the time to reflect on our accomplishments and successes and acknowledging the unique talents and qualities we bring to the table. By focusing on our strengths and building on them, we can develop inner confidence that will radiate outwards and make us more charismatic.

Another important aspect of confidence is handling failure or rejection with grace and resilience. No one is perfect, and we are all bound to experience setbacks or disappointments at some point. However, those who are truly confident can take these setbacks in stride, learn from them, and move on without dwelling on them or letting them undermine their self-belief.

One way to build confidence is to set achievable goals and work towards them systematically. By breaking down larger goals into smaller, more manageable steps, we can make a sense of accomplishment and momentum that will help us develop confidence and self-assurance.

It's worth noting that confidence is not the same as arrogance or egotism. The strengths or accomplishments of others do not threaten a truly confident person, but rather sees them as opportunities to learn and grow. By embracing a growth mindset and cultivating an attitude of curiosity and openness, we can become more confident and charismatic and build stronger connections with those around us.

In conclusion, developing charisma is not about changing who you are but enhancing and highlighting your positive qualities. By practicing techniques such as active listening, storytelling, humor, and cultivating confidence, you can become more charismatic and build deeper connections with those around you.

MICROEXPRESSIONS ARE WORTH A THOUSAND WORDS

Have you ever been in a conversation and noticed a fleeting expression on the other person's face that didn't quite match what they were saying? That's a micro expression, a brief and involuntary facial expression that reveals a person's true emotions. In this chapter, we'll explore the intricacies of microexpressions, including what they are, how to recognize them, the feelings behind them, techniques for responding to micro expressions, and the role of micro expressions in building rapport.

WHAT ARE MICROEXPRESSIONS?

In today's world, communication is not only about what we say but also how we say it. Sometimes, the smallest facial expression can reveal a wealth of information about a person's thoughts and feelings. These fleeting facial expressions are known as microexpressions.

Microexpressions are tiny facial expressions that occur involuntarily and only last for a fraction of a second. They often reveal an emotion that the person is trying to conceal but cannot completely hide. These expressions can provide valuable insights into what a person truly feels, even when trying to hide it.

Some common microexpressions include a slight raising of the eyebrows, a subtle furrowing of the brow, a fleeting smile, or a quick frown. These expressions happen so quickly that they can be difficult to detect with the naked eye. However, with some practice, you can learn to recognize these tiny facial expressions and use them to your advantage in various situations.

One of the most significant benefits of recognizing microexpressions is that it can help you understand people better. For example, if someone expresses a negative emotion like anger, sadness or disgust, you can adjust your communication style to make them feel more comfortable. You can also use your knowledge of microexpressions to identify when someone is lying or hiding something from you.

Another benefit of understanding microexpressions is that it can help you become more empathetic and understanding. By learning to recognize the emotions behind microexpressions, you can develop a deeper level of compassion and empathy toward others. This can help you build stronger relationships and create a better understanding of the people around you.

Overall, microexpressions are an important aspect of communication that can reveal a wealth of information about a person's true thoughts and feelings. By recognizing and responding to these tiny facial expressions, you can become a better communicator and build stronger relationships with the people around you.

HOW TO RECOGNIZE MICROEXPRESSIONS

Microexpressions are fleeting facial expressions that last only a fraction of a second. These expressions are so brief that the naked eye often misses them. However, if you can recognize them, they can provide valuable insight into a person's emotions and intentions.

To recognize microexpressions, it's important to start by paying close attention to a person's face. Look for subtle changes in their facial muscles, such as the tightening of the lips or the narrowing of the eyes. These small changes can indicate a person's true emotions, even if they are trying to hide them.

It's also important to pay attention to the context in which the microexpression occurs. For example, if a person suddenly looks angry during a conversation, it could indicate frustration with what you are saying. If they suddenly look sad, it could mean they are upset about something you've said or done.

Another important factor to consider is timing. Microexpressions often occur very quickly, so it's important to be observant and quick to pick up on them. It's also important to note that microexpressions can occur in clusters. For example, a person may show several microexpressions of anger or frustration, indicating that they are becoming increasingly upset.

To further hone your ability to recognize microexpressions, you can practice with a partner or by watching videos of people displaying different emotions. Look for the small, subtle changes in their facial expressions and try to identify the feelings behind them.

Overall, recognizing microexpressions can be a valuable tool in building rapport and understanding the emotions of those around you. By paying close attention to a person's facial expressions and context, you can gain valuable insights into their thoughts and feelings.

THE EMOTIONS BEHIND MICROEXPRESSIONS

Microexpressions are fleeting facial expressions that reveal a person's true emotions, even when they are trying to conceal them. Although they only last for a fraction of a second, microexpressions can be very revealing and provide valuable insight into a person's thoughts and feelings.

The emotions behind microexpressions are diverse and can range from joy to anger, fear, disgust, surprise, and sadness. These universal emotions can be observed in people from all cultures and backgrounds.

Joy is a positive emotion often associated with smiling, a facial expression involving the lips and the eyes. When a person experiences joy, their mouth will curve upward, and their eyes will narrow and wrinkle at the corners.

Anger is a negative emotion often associated with a furrowed brow, flared nostrils, and a tight-lipped expression. When a person experiences anger, their eyebrows will pull together, and their mouth will form a straight line.

Fear is another negative emotion often associated with widened eyes, a raised brow, and a slightly open mouth. When a person experiences fear, their eyes will open wider, and their pupils will dilate, making them appear larger.

Disgust is a negative emotion often associated with a wrinkled nose, a furrowed brow, and an open mouth. When a person experiences disgust, their nose will wrinkle, and their lips will pull back, exposing their teeth.

Surprise is a neutral emotion often associated with widened eyes and a dropped jaw. When a person experiences surprise, their eyebrows will raise, and their mouth will open slightly.

Sadness is a negative emotion often associated with a downward curve of the mouth, drooping eyelids, and a furrowed brow. When a person experiences sadness, their mouth will curve downward, and their eyes will appear heavy and downcast.

Understanding the emotions behind microexpressions can help us to understand better the people we interact with and build stronger relationships with them. By recognizing and responding appropriately to microexpressions, we can become more empathetic, which can enhance our ability to connect with others and build rapport.

TECHNIQUES FOR RESPONDING TO MICROEXPRESSIONS

Once you've learned how to recognize microexpressions, the next step is to develop techniques for responding to them. Here are some strategies that you can use to respond effectively to micro expressions:

1.   Be present and attentive: The first step in responding to microexpressions is to be fully present and attentive to the person you are communicating with. Pay close attention to their facial expressions and body language to better understand their feelings.

2.   Use active listening: Active listening involves hearing what the other person is saying and understanding their nonverbal cues. When responding to microexpressions, actively listen to the person and validate their emotions by acknowledging them.

3.   Respond empathetically: Responding empathetically to micro expressions can go a long way in building rapport and strengthening relationships. Let the person know that you understand their feelings and that you are there to support them.

4.   Clarify your understanding: If you are unsure what a microexpression means, don't be afraid to ask the person to clarify their emotions. This can help you better understand the situation and respond appropriately.

5.   Adjust your communication: Once you have responded to a microexpression, adjust your communication style accordingly. For example, if the person appears upset or angry, you may want to speak calmly and reassuringly to help de-escalate the situation.

In conclusion, responding to microexpressions is an important skill for effective communication and building strong relationships. By being present and attentive, using active listening, responding empathetically, clarifying your understanding, and adjusting your communication, you can effectively respond to microexpressions and improve your communication skills.

THE ROLE OF MICROEXPRESSIONS IN BUILDING RAPPORT

When you can detect microexpressions, you can show empathy and understanding toward the other person. This helps build trust and create a stronger bond between you and the person you're communicating with. Additionally, it can also help you avoid misunderstandings, as you can pick up on subtle cues that may indicate that the person is feeling something other than what they are saying.

Recognizing microexpressions can also give you an advantage in negotiations or sales, as you can read the other person's emotions and adjust your approach accordingly. For example, if you notice a microexpression of frustration, you can change your tone or approach to alleviate their frustration and make them more receptive to your message.

However, it's important to note that microexpressions should be cautiously used. It's easy to misinterpret a microexpression, and it's important to consider the context in which it appears.

Additionally, focusing too much on microexpressions can lead to over-analysis and may cause you to miss the bigger picture.

In conclusion, understanding and utilizing microexpressions can be valuable in building rapport, improving communication, and enhancing your social and professional relationships. By learning how to recognize microexpressions and respond appropriately, you can gain a deeper understanding of the emotions of those around you and create stronger connections with the people in your life.

TWO MAGIC WORDS FOR UNENDING CONVERSATIONS

Have you ever found yourself in a conversation that feels like it's coming to an end? Maybe you're struggling to think of what to say next or worried the other person is losing interest. Fear not because two magic words can keep the conversation going: "Tell me."

This chapter will explore the power of "tell me" and how to use it to keep a conversation flowing effortlessly. We'll provide you with strategies for using "tell me" effectively, tips for adapting it to different situations, and explain the importance of active listening in making the most of this powerful tool.

WHAT IS THE POWER OF "TELL ME"?

When keeping a conversation going, "Tell me" can be two of the most powerful words in your arsenal. These simple words can encourage others to share their thoughts, feelings, and experiences, leading to deeper and more meaningful conversations.

The power of "tell me" lies in its ability to show genuine interest in what the other person has to say. When you ask someone to tell you something, you invite them to share a part of themselves with you. This can help build trust and rapport and make the other person feel valued and heard.

In addition to showing interest, "tell me" can also steer the conversation in a certain direction. For example, if you're trying to get to know someone better, you can use "tell me" to ask about their hobbies, interests, or background. Or, if you're trying to resolve a conflict or solve a problem, you can use "tell me" to encourage the other person to share their perspective and ideas.

One of the key benefits of using "tell me" is that it can help to keep the conversation flowing. When you ask someone a question or make a statement, there's a chance that the conversation could stall or come to a halt. However, when you use "tell me," you give the other person an open-ended prompt that invites them to continue talking. This can help to prevent awkward silences or lulls in the conversation.

Another benefit of using "tell me" is that it can help to foster active listening. When you ask someone to tell you something, you signal that you are ready and willing to listen to what they say. This can encourage you to pay closer attention to their words, tone of voice, and body language, which can help you to understand their perspective and feelings better.

Overall, the power of "tell me" lies in creating deeper, more meaningful conversations. By showing genuine interest, steering the conversation, and fostering active listening, "tell me" can help to build trust, rapport, and understanding between people.

HOW TO USE "TELL ME" TO KEEP A CONVERSATION GOING

The phrase "tell me" is a powerful tool for keeping a conversation going, especially when you're struggling to say something. When used effectively, "tell me" can lead to deeper and more meaningful conversations.

One of the ways to use "tell me" to keep a conversation going is by asking open-ended questions. Open-ended questions require more than a simple yes or no answer and can lead to more detailed responses. For example, instead of asking, "Did you have a good weekend?" which can be answered with a simple "yes" or "no," try asking, "Tell me about your weekend." This encourages the other person to share more details about their weekend, leading to a more in-depth conversation.

Another way to use "tell me" to keep a conversation going is to show genuine interest in the other person's thoughts and feelings. For example, if someone tells you they recently started a new job, you can respond by saying, "Tell me more about your new job. What do you like about it?" This shows that you are genuinely interested in their experiences and are willing to listen to them.

Using "tell me" can also help steer the conversation towards topics the other person is interested in. For example, if you're talking to someone about their hobbies and they mention that they enjoy playing music, you can say, "Tell me more about your music. What kind of instruments do you play?" This allows the other person to talk about something they are passionate about and can lead to a more engaging conversation.

It's important to note that "tell me" effectively requires active listening. Pay attention to what the other person is saying and respond with follow-up questions or comments to keep the conversation flowing. Also, be sure to use "tell me" in a natural and conversational tone rather than as a scripted or robotic question.

In summary, "tell me" can be a powerful tool for keeping a conversation going. You can create a more engaging and meaningful conversation by asking open-ended questions, showing genuine interest, and steering the conversation towards the other person's interests. Just remember to actively listen and use "tell me" in a natural tone to make the conversation flow smoothly.

STRATEGIES FOR USING "TELL ME" EFFECTIVELY

"tell me" is an effective way to keep a conversation going, but it's not enough to ask the other person to share more. Here are some strategies for using "tell me" effectively:

1.   Be genuine: When you use "tell me," it's important to be sincere and genuinely interested in what the other person says. Don't use it as a way to fill awkward silences or to show off your conversational skills.

2.   Follow up: Once the other person has shared something with you, follow up with a question or comment. This shows that you were listening and interested in hearing more.

3.   Use open-ended questions: Rather than asking yes or no questions, use open-ended questions encouraging the other person to share more. For example, instead of asking, "Do you like your job?" ask, "What do you enjoy?"

4.   Be attentive: Pay attention to the other person's body language and tone of voice. This can give you clues about their feelings and what they might want to discuss.

5.   Avoid interrupting: Let the other person finish their thoughts before jumping in with your opinion or story. Interrupting can be rude and make the other person feel unheard.

6.   Show empathy: When the other person shares something personal or emotional, show empathy by acknowledging their feelings and offering support or encouragement.

Using these strategies, you can effectively use "tell me" to keep a conversation going and deepen your connection with the other person.

TIPS FOR ADAPTING "TELL ME" TO DIFFERENT SITUATIONS

"Tell me" is a powerful tool to keep conversations going, but adapting it to different situations is important to make it effective. This section will explore tips for adapting "tell me" to different situations.

1.   Social Situations:

In social situations, being mindful of the other person's comfort level is important. Use "tell me" in a friendly, non-invasive manner. For example, "Tell me more about your weekend" or "Tell me about your favorite hobby." Avoid using "tell me" in a confrontational way that might make the other person uncomfortable.

2.   Professional Situations:

In professional situations, it is important to respect the other person's time and professional boundaries. Use "tell me" in a way that is related to the topic at hand. For example, "Tell me more about your experience in project management" or "Tell me about your thoughts on the current market trends." Avoid using "tell me" in a way that might appear prying or unprofessional.

3.   Personal Situations:

In personal situations, it is important to be empathetic and understanding. Use "tell me" to show that you are genuinely interested in the other person's thoughts and feelings. For example, "Tell me how you're feeling about the recent changes in your life" or "Tell me about your favorite childhood memory." Avoid using "tell me" in a way that might make the other person feel uncomfortable or judged.

4.   Cross-Cultural Situations:

It is important to be aware of cultural differences and norms in cross-cultural situations. Use "tell me" in a way that is respectful of the other person's culture and beliefs. For example, "Tell me more about your cultural traditions" or "Your thoughts on the intersection of culture and identity." Avoid using "tell me" in a way that might come across as insensitive or disrespectful of the other person's cultural background.

In summary, adopting "tell me" to different situations requires awareness of the other person's comfort level, professional boundaries, personal feelings, and cultural norms. Using "tell me" in a respectful and empathetic manner can help build rapport and create meaningful connections. The role of active listening is also crucial in adapting "tell me" effectively to different situations, as it allows us to respond appropriately to the other person's thoughts and feelings.

THE ROLE OF ACTIVE LISTENING IN "TELL ME"

Active listening is an essential component of effective communication and is especially important when using the phrase "tell me" to keep a conversation going. Active listening is more than just hearing what the other person is saying; it involves fully engaging with the speaker and demonstrating an interest in what they have to say.

One key aspect of active listening is giving the speaker your full attention. This means minimizing distractions, such as putting away your phone, turning off the television, and focusing solely on the speaker. By doing so, you are showing the speaker that you value what they say and that you are invested in the conversation.

Another important aspect of active listening is paraphrasing or summarizing what the speaker has said. This shows that you have understood their point and allows for clarification if needed. When using "tell me" to keep a conversation going, it is important to use active listening techniques like paraphrasing to encourage the speaker to continue sharing their thoughts and ideas.

Active listening also involves nonverbal cues such as nodding, maintaining eye contact, and using appropriate facial expressions to convey interest and understanding. By doing so, you are sending a message to the speaker that you are fully engaged in the conversation and interested in what they have to say.

In addition, active listening requires an open mind and a willingness to learn from the other person. This means setting aside preconceived notions or biases and being open to new ideas and perspectives. When using "tell me" to keep a conversation going, it is important to approach the conversation with a curious and open mindset, ready to learn and grow from the other person's experiences and insights.

In summary, active listening in "tell me" is crucial for building rapport and keeping a conversation going. By fully engaging with the speaker, paraphrasing and summarizing their points, using nonverbal cues to convey interest and understanding, and approaching the discussion with an open mind, you can use "tell me" to its full potential and create meaningful and lasting connections with others.

In conclusion, "tell me" is a powerful tool that can keep a conversation going indefinitely. You can build stronger relationships and make meaningful connections by showing a genuine interest in what the other person has to say. With the strategies and tips in this chapter, you can use "tell me" effectively and become a skilled conversationalist.

UNDERSTAND THE THREE LEVELS OF RAPPORT

Building rapport is essential to establishing connections with others in personal or professional settings. However, not all rapport is created equal. In this chapter, we'll explore the three levels of connection and provide you with strategies for building and maintaining them, including techniques for moving from surface level to deeper connection, the role of empathy in building rapport, and how to use rapport to achieve your goals.

THE DIFFERENT LEVELS OF RAPPORT

Building rapport is essential for successful communication and creating strong relationships with others. However, it's not always easy to establish and maintain connection. Understanding the different levels of rapport can help you identify where you are in a relationship and what steps you can take to deepen it.

First Level

The first level of rapport is the surface level. This is the initial level of interaction when you first meet someone or are still getting to know them. At this level, the conversation tends to be superficial and focused on getting to know the other person's interests and hobbies. It's important to establish this level of rapport first, as it creates a foundation for further interaction and builds a sense of familiarity.

Second Level

The second level of rapport is the personal level. This level goes beyond the surface level and involves deeper, more private conversations. At this level, you may discuss topics such as values, beliefs, and life experiences. It's important to approach these conversations with empathy and an open mind, as they require vulnerability and trust.

Third Level

The third and deepest level of rapport is the intimate level. This level involves a high degree of trust and emotional connection. You may share personal stories and experiences at this level, and the conversation becomes more authentic and vulnerable. It's important to approach this level with sensitivity and respect, as it requires high emotional intelligence and empathy.

Building rapport requires active listening, empathy, and a genuine interest in the other person. To move from one level of rapport to the next, paying attention to the other person's cues and responding appropriately is important. This means being present at the moment, asking open-ended questions, and showing a genuine interest in what the other person is saying.

By understanding the different levels of rapport and how to move between them, you can create deeper and more meaningful connections with the people in your life. Remember that building rapport takes time and effort, but the rewards are ultimately worth it.

HOW TO BUILD AND MAINTAIN RAPPORT

Building and maintaining rapport is a crucial component of effective communication. When people feel that they have a good connection with someone, they are more likely to trust them and be open to their ideas. It can also help to establish a positive and productive working relationship with colleagues, clients, and customers.

There are several ways to build and maintain rapport with others. Here are some effective strategies:

1.   Show genuine interest: To build rapport, showing genuine interest in the other person is essential. Ask them questions about themselves, their interests, and their work. Listen actively to their answers and respond thoughtfully. When you show interest in what someone says, they feel valued and respected, which can help build rapport.

2.   Find common ground: Another way to build rapport is to find common ground with the other person. This can be anything from a shared hobby to a similar work experience. When you find common ground, it creates a sense of connection and can help to build rapport.

3.   Be authentic: People can sense when someone is not original, so it's important to be genuine in your interactions. Be true to yourself and let your personality shine through. When you

are accurate, people are more likely to trust you and feel comfortable around you, which can help to build rapport.

4.   Use positive body language: Body language can be a powerful tool for building rapport. Use open and relaxed body language, such as uncrossed arms and legs, to show you are approachable and open to conversation. Make eye contact and smile to show you are engaged and interested in the conversation.

5.   Follow up: Once you have established rapport with someone, it's important to maintain it. Follow up with the person regularly through email, phone, or in-person conversations. This can help to maintain the connection and keep the rapport strong.

Building and maintaining rapport takes time and effort, but it's worth it. Having a good rapport with someone can help establish trust, increase collaboration, and achieve your goals more effectively. By showing genuine interest, finding common ground, being authentic, using positive body language, and following up, you can build and maintain rapport with others.

TECHNIQUES FOR MOVING FROM SURFACE LEVEL TO DEEPER RAPPORT

Creating and maintaining rapport with others is essential to building strong relationships. However, building rapport takes time, effort, and the ability to move beyond surface-level interactions. Here are some techniques to help you move from surface level to deeper rapport:

1.   Ask open-ended questions: One of the best ways to move beyond small talk is by asking open-ended questions. Instead of asking yes or no questions, ask questions that require the other person to elaborate on their thoughts, feelings, and experiences. For example, instead of asking, "Do you like your job?" ask, "What do you enjoy most?" This will encourage the other person to share more information and help you to gain a deeper understanding of them.

2.   Active listening: Active listening is the art of paying full attention to what someone is saying without judgment or interruption. When you actively listen to someone, you show them that you are interested in what they have to say and value their perspective. This, in turn, creates a deeper sense of connection and can help build rapport.

3.   Share personal experiences: Sharing personal experiences can be an effective way to build rapport with someone. By sharing your own experiences, you show the other person that you trust them and are willing to be vulnerable. This can encourage them to open up and share their experiences, which can help deepen the relationship.

4.   Find common ground: Finding common ground with someone is an excellent way to build rapport. Look for shared interests, experiences, or beliefs that you can discuss. This can help create a sense of connection and lead to more meaningful conversations.

5.   Pay attention to body language: Body language can be a powerful indicator of how someone is feeling. By paying attention to their body language, you can better understand their emotions, thoughts, and feelings. This can help you adjust your approach and connect with them more deeply.

Overall, building rapport is about connecting with someone on a deeper level. Using these techniques to move beyond surface-level interactions, you can build stronger, more meaningful relationships with others.

THE ROLE OF EMPATHY IN BUILDING RAPPORT

Empathy is a key factor in building and maintaining rapport with others. It is the ability to put yourself in someone else's shoes and understand their thoughts, feelings, and perspectives. When you demonstrate empathy towards someone, you show that you care about their well-being, which can foster trust and deepen your relationship.

One way to show empathy is through active listening. When you listen attentively to someone, you demonstrate that you value their perspective and are interested in understanding their point of view. You can also show empathy through nonverbal cues such as eye contact, nodding, and another body language. These nonverbal cues can help convey that you are present at the moment and focused on what the other person is saying.

Another way to demonstrate empathy is using language that reflects your understanding of the other person's perspective. For example, you can use statements such as "I can see why you would feel that way" or "It sounds like you're going through a tough time" to show that you understand and acknowledge their feelings.

It's also important to remember that empathy is not just about understanding the other person's emotions and feelings but also about taking action to help them. For example, if someone is going through a difficult time, you can offer to help them in any way you can. This can be as simple as listening to them, offering advice, or providing practical assistance.

In addition to building rapport, empathy can also help you resolve conflicts and prevent misunderstandings. When you approach a disagreement with empathy, you can better understand the other person's point of view and work towards a solution that benefits everyone involved.

Overall, empathy plays a crucial role in building and maintaining rapport. Demonstrating empathy towards others can foster trust, deepen relationships, and create a more positive and supportive environment.

HOW TO USE RAPPORT TO ACHIEVE YOUR GOALS

In building rapport, the ultimate goal is to establish a connection with someone and achieve a certain objective. This objective could be personal or professional, and the strength of your rapport will determine the likelihood of achieving it. Here are some techniques to use rapport to achieve your goals:

1.   Identify your goal: Before you begin building rapport, it is essential to identify the objects you want to achieve. This could be anything from gaining a new client to negotiating a raise at work. Once you have identified your goal, you can tailor your rapport-building efforts toward achieving that objective.

2.   Focus on the other person's needs: To build strong rapport, you must demonstrate genuine interest in the other person. This means actively listening to them, asking questions, and responding thoughtfully. By understanding the other person's needs, you can tailor your communication to address those needs and ultimately achieve your goal.

3.   Highlight shared values: Finding common ground is a powerful way to build rapport. By highlighting shared values, you can create a sense of unity and establish a stronger connection with the other person. This can also help to align your goals with theirs and create a mutually beneficial outcome.

4.   Use persuasive language: When trying to achieve a goal through rapport, it's essential to use compelling speech. This means framing your communication to appeal to the other person's emotions and desires. Using clear speech, you can make a compelling case for your objective and increase the likelihood of success.

5.   Be persistent but respectful: Building strong rapport takes time, and you may encounter setbacks. It's essential to be continued in your efforts while respecting the other person's boundaries and needs. Remember that rapport-building is a two-

way street, and finding a balance between pushing for your objective and maintaining a positive relationship is crucial.

Understanding the different levels of rapport is crucial in achieving your goals through communication. By identifying your objective, focusing on the other person's needs, highlighting shared values, using persuasive language, and being persistent yet respectful, you can use rapport to achieve your goals effectively.

In conclusion, understanding the three levels of rapport and how to build and maintain them can significantly impact your personal and professional relationships. You can establish more meaningful and long-lasting connections with others by utilizing techniques for moving from surface level to deeper rapport, demonstrating empathy, and using rapport to achieve your goals.

BUILDING AND MAINTAINING RELATIONSHIPS

Relationships are an integral part of human existence. We all need people with whom we can share our joys and sorrows, successes and failures. Building and maintaining relationships takes effort, but it is worth it for the benefits of strong and meaningful connections. This chapter will explore the importance of relationships, how to maintain existing relationships, techniques for building new relationships, the power of gratitude in relationships, tips for repairing damaged relationships, and how to use rapport to achieve your goals.

THE IMPORTANCE OF RELATIONSHIPS

Relationships are crucial to our well-being. Whether personal or professional, relationships provide us with a sense of belonging and support. We need people in our lives who can help us navigate life's challenges and celebrate our achievements. Healthy relationships also help us build resilience and increase our happiness and satisfaction with life.

HOW TO MAINTAIN EXISTING RELATIONSHIPS

Maintaining existing relationships takes time and effort. It requires consistent communication, mutual respect, and a willingness to compromise. To maintain a relationship, it's important to show interest in the other person's life, actively listen to what they say, and support their goals and aspirations.

Remembering important dates like birthdays and anniversaries can also help strengthen the bond between two people.

TECHNIQUES FOR BUILDING NEW RELATIONSHIPS

Building new relationships can be intimidating but essential for personal and professional growth. To create new relationships, start by being approachable and open to meeting new people. Attend social events, join clubs or groups with similar interests, and engage in activities where you can meet like-minded individuals. Take the initiative to strike up conversations and find common ground with others.

THE POWER OF GRATITUDE IN RELATIONSHIPS

Expressing gratitude in relationships can go a long way in strengthening the bond between two people. A simple "thank you," or note of appreciation can make someone feel valued and appreciated. Regularly expressing gratitude can help create a positive and nurturing environment where people feel comfortable sharing their thoughts and feelings.

TIPS FOR REPAIRING DAMAGED RELATIONSHIPS

Relationships can face challenges and setbacks. When things go wrong, it's essential to take steps to repair the damage. Start by acknowledging the problem and taking responsibility for your part in the situation. Apologize sincerely and listen to the other person's point of view. Work together to find a solution that works for both parties.

HOW TO USE RAPPORT TO ACHIEVE YOUR GOALS

Rapport is essential in building and maintaining relationships. It helps establish trust and mutual understanding, which can be especially useful in achieving your goals. To use rapport effectively, start by actively listening to the other person and finding common ground. Pay attention to their body language and tone of voice to better understand their perspective. Use this information to establish a connection and work together towards a shared goal.

In conclusion, building and maintaining relationships is essential for personal and professional growth. It requires effort, but the benefits of strong and meaningful connections are worth it. Use the techniques outlined in this chapter to build rapport, express gratitude, and repair damaged relationships. Remember, relationships are a two-way street, and it's up to both parties to put in the effort to make them thrive.

CONCLUSION

As we end this book, we hope you have gained valuable insights into the world of communication. We have covered many topics, from the importance of active listening to building and maintaining relationships.

Effective communication is essential to every aspect of our lives, from personal relationships to professional careers. Communicating effectively can make all the difference in achieving our goals and living a fulfilling life.

We have explored how to improve our communication skills by understanding the different levels of rapport, the power of empathy, and the role of active listening. We have also covered techniques for building and maintaining relationships, such as expressing gratitude, repairing damaged relationships, and using rapport to achieve our goals.

Remember that communication is not just about speaking; it also involves listening, understanding, and connecting with others. It's about creating a safe and supportive environment for everyone to express themselves, share ideas, and work together towards a common goal.

As you go out into the world, we encourage you to continue to practice and improve your communication skills. Don't be afraid to ask for feedback, seek opportunities to learn and grow, and remember to approach every conversation with empathy and an open mind.

In conclusion, we hope this book has been a valuable resource for improving your communication skills and relationships. Thank you for reading, and we wish you all the best in your communication journey.

Dear Esteemed Reader,

Thank you for choosing "Talk with Power to Anyone" to enhance your communication skills and transform your social life! Your journey to confident communication begins here.

Share Your Insights (Optional):

Your feedback holds immense value. If you found the book helpful, please take a moment to share your thoughts by leaving a review. Your insights motivate me to continue creating content that empowers and uplifts.

Scan Here to Leave Your Review

As a gesture of appreciation, I'm delighted to present you with an exclusive bonus:

Free Audiobook Version

Immerse yourself in the content with our narrated audiobook version. Enhance your learning experience and reinforce the principles of powerful communication.

Access Your Complimentary Bonus Now!

Thank you for being a valued reader. Here's to unlocking the secrets of confident communication and building genuine connections!

Best Regards,

Isabel Pierce

www.ingramcontent.com/pod-product-compliance
Lightning Source LLC
Chambersburg PA
CBHW050727260726
48661CB00001B/104